I0800854

IMAGES
of America

GREEKS OF WORCESTER

This postcard depicts the Temple of Hephaestus in Athens, sometimes erroneously referred to as Theseion. In Ancient Greece, the temple was dedicated to Hephaestus, the god of fire, volcanoes, and the crafts that required fire. Hephaestus was, according to Homer, the son of Zeus and Hera and husband to Aphrodite. From the seventh century AD to 1834, the temple served as a Greek Orthodox Church. In 1834, it became a museum. (Author's collection.)

On the Cover: St. Spyridon Greek Orthodox Church officially opened on Palm Sunday, April 13, 1952. In this photograph with Worcester's historic Elm Park in the background, altar boys lead the procession of the church choir, clergy, and faithful from the parish house to the steps of the church along Russell Street. They hold various icons as well as the flag of Greece and the flag of the United States, which had 48 stars at the time. (WHM.)

IMAGES
of America

Greeks of Worcester

Christopher J. Helali

ARCADIA
PUBLISHING

ISBN 978-1-4671-0813-3

Published by Arcadia Publishing
Charleston, South Carolina

Printed in the United States of America

Library of Congress Control Number: 2022938574

For all general information, please contact Arcadia Publishing:
Telephone 843-853-2070
Fax 843-853-0044
E-mail sales@arcadiapublishing.com
For customer service and orders:
Toll-Free 1-888-313-2665

Visit us on the Internet at www.arcadiapublishing.com

For Yiayia, Pappou, and Theio Yiorgo.

Honor and glory to the heroic fighters of EAM-ELAS-EPON, OPLA, DSE, and the Communist Party of Greece (KKE).

CONTENTS

ACKNOWLEDGMENTS

The research for this book began shortly before the outbreak of COVID-19. The pandemic impacted everyone in our community. We remember those in Worcester's Greek community that passed away over the past few years, including my Theia Helen Rougas and my brother's *nouna*, Theia Ekaterini Singas. May their memories be eternal.

None of this would have been possible without the support and resources provided by Wendy Essery, library and archive manager at the Worcester Historical Museum (WHM). Wendy and the staff at the museum have earned my immeasurable gratitude for their hard work on this project.

Thank you to my title manager at Arcadia Publishing, Stacia Bannerman, for her support, guidance, and patience. Thank you to the staff at Dartmouth College's Jones Media Lab and Peter Allen of the Evans Map Room who assisted me in scanning and digitizing the photographs. Thank you to Jody and Angie Walsh, George and Helen Panagiotopoulos, Demetrios Koutoulas, Katherine Peepas, Dr. Matthew Panagiotu, Kathryn Tsandikos, Tasos Anastasakis, Prof. Dimitrios Konstadakopulos, Eleni Alexakis, Michelangelo Bevilacqua, Theia Grigoria and Yiayia Maria Katelani, Theia Paraskevi Kasidakos, Theio Vasilios Alexiou, and my cousins Konstantinos and Nikolaos Alexiou of Athens, Greece, for all your help and support.

Because I grew up in the Greek community of Worcester, this book has been a three-year labor of love. St. Spyridon, where I was baptized, served as an altar boy, and received my initial theological training, is a deeply and profoundly meaningful sacred space and community for me.

I want to thank my *yiayia*, *pappou*, and all my elders and ancestors whose boundless love shaped who I am today. They cultivated in me a love for family, our culture, and our traditions. To my mom, Paraskevi, and *baba-jan*, Davood, for your endless love, support, and guidance throughout my life. To my brother, Peter, for your love. To my wife, Amanda, thank you for all your love, support, and encouragement not just on this project but in everything. Finally, to my children Sojourner, Theodore, and Mina—this is now part of your history.

Numerous images in this volume appear courtesy of the Worcester Historical Museum (WHM), Jody Walsh (JW), and the Helali, Kasidakos, and Nikolinakos Family Archive (HKN).

INTRODUCTION

In March 1821, the Maniates, historically autonomous and self-governing, declared war on the Ottoman Empire. Under the command of Petrobey Mavromichalis, the Maniates laid siege to the Messenian town of Kalamata and, within a few days, had liberated it. The Greek War of Independence had begun. The revolution and subsequent independence of Greece reshaped the political order in Europe and changed the course of world history.

The enthusiasm of the early years of independence quickly dissipated as political divisions, economic crises, war, and relations between the Great Powers paralyzed Greece. While the Greek state attempted various reforms and enacted policies aimed at industrialization and education, Greece remained an impoverished nation. Most members of Greece's population were peasants who lived in rural areas and relied on subsistence agriculture to survive.

Emigration in the latter part of the 19th century provided opportunities for those fortunate enough to leave Greece. In the 1890s, Greeks began arriving in Worcester, Massachusetts, mainly from the Peloponnesus region, since other regions—including Epirus, Macedonia, Thessaly, and Crete—were still under Ottoman occupation. This would change in the aftermath of the Second Balkan War, which ended in 1913 with the Treaty of Bucharest ceding large portions of Epirus, Macedonia, and Crete to Greece.

Thus, in the first few decades of the 20th century, the majority of the Greeks who came to Worcester arrived from Northern Greece, mainly from the region of Epirus. The ongoing collapse of the Ottoman Empire led to a wave of emigration from recently liberated areas.

Greeks in the United States faced prejudice at the hands of various right-wing groups that promoted nativism and racism. The Ku Klux Klan (KKK) launched a terror campaign against Greeks in many parts of the country. In response, the American Hellenic Educational Progressive Association (AHEPA) was formed not only to combat the KKK but also to push for the full Americanization of the Greek-American community. Given the de jure racial segregation in the United States, Greek-Americans sought to differentiate themselves from other racialized minority groups, paving the way toward "whiteness."

Anti-immigration sentiments in the United States and the need to stop "undesirable" populations from coming to the country led to changes in immigration laws that culminated in two important pieces of legislation. The Emergency Quota Act of 1921 put in place a quota system to stem the tide of immigration, mainly from Southern and Eastern Europe. The Immigration Act of 1924, including the Asian Exclusion Act and National Origins Act, further strengthened immigration restrictions and created the US Border Patrol. The legislation had profound impacts on Greek immigration. Greek immigrants had been arriving in the thousands before the legislation, but after it passed, only a few hundred were coming to the United States per year.

However, the Greeks in Worcester were already establishing the foundations of a thriving community. Most of the arrivals from Greece were young bachelors or married men who had come over in search of work. Through hard labor, many saved enough money to bring their families or return to Greece to marry and bring over families. Greeks worked in various industries but primarily as laborers in factories and mills or the food industry. Others were street peddlers, merchants, bootblacks, clerks, tailors, barbers, shoemakers, and pin boys. They lived together in boardinghouses and cooperative living arrangements at first. Some Greeks, driven by an entrepreneurial spirit, established themselves as businessmen, hiring other Greeks to support the community.

The Greeks of Worcester, navigating a complex new nation, sought to build a sacred space where they could carry out their religious rituals and rites in accordance with their Eastern Orthodox faith. Prior to the establishment of a Greek Orthodox church in the area, priests from other parishes would perform sacraments and liturgies. Greeks in Worcester would perform their sacraments at St. George's Antiochian (Syrian) Orthodox Church.

On October 15, 1914, the Greek Orthodox Community of Worcester was officially established with an agreed-upon constitution. The Greek community performed church services at Beaver Hall at 69 Grafton Street. Meetings were held at 9 Bartlett Street, 126 Green Street, and the Ancient Order of Hibernians (AOH) Hall at 26 Trumbull Street.

Eventually, the community was able to organize into a legal corporation and obtain a charter from the Commonwealth of Massachusetts on September 26, 1916. The new church was named after the fourth-century bishop of Trimythous, St. Spyridon, who participated in the First Ecumenical Council of Nicaea. St. Spyridon was chosen because his incorruptible relics are located on Kerkyra (Corfu), just across from Epirus, where many of the Greeks of Worcester came from. Additionally, St. Spyridon's feast day fell on Christmas on the old calendar, meaning laborers would not lose a working day.

Political divisions in Greece, as well as local rivalries, led to factionalism in the Greek community. In 1924, construction began on St. Spyridon Greek Orthodox Church on Orange Street, culminating in the church's consecration on May 3, 1925. Armenian architect Hachadoor Sarkis Demoorjian, whose portfolio includes the Annunciation Greek Orthodox Cathedral in Boston, designed the church.

In the mid-20th century, war in Europe and the Axis occupation of Greece, which was divided between Germany, Italy, and Bulgaria, loomed over Worcester's Greek community. The community organized relief efforts and humanitarian aid. Five young Greek-American men of Worcester lost their lives in World War II. World War II, the Greek Civil War, political instability, the military dictatorship, and pogroms of Greeks in Istanbul all contributed to additional waves of immigration from the 1950s through the 1970s.

The need for a larger church due to the growing Greek community led to the purchase of a lot on Russell Street. A new St. Spyridon church was designed by architect Christopher Kantianis. Construction commenced on November 12, 1950. The church opened on April 13, 1952, and was officially consecrated on May 30, 1954. The church's community center was completed and opened on May 7, 1965. On December 12, 1985, St. Spyridon Greek Orthodox Church was elevated by Metropolitan Methodios of Boston and became St. Spyridon Greek Orthodox Cathedral.

St. Spyridon has also witnessed history under its roof. On September 9, 1965, the first formal and sanctioned dialogue between Orthodox and Catholic theologians since the Council of Florence in 1439 (approximately 15 years before the collapse of the Byzantine Empire) was held in the Tonna Room.

The Greek community of Worcester continues to thrive. It hosts a successful biennial festival, formed the Hellenic Arts Society, provides food to the needy with a food pantry, helps organize Sunday of Orthodoxy and Presanctified liturgies with other area Orthodox churches, and helps maintain the Holy Trinity Nursing and Rehabilitation Center. There have been recent upgrades to the community center, renovations of the church and its facilities, and expanded parking.

The Greeks of Worcester have made—and continue to make—a lasting impact on the city and region with their culture, traditions, religion, and labor. They are trailblazers and innovators excelling in education, the arts, science, medicine, law, business, and politics. Hellenism and Orthodoxy, the two beacons that guided the first immigrants, continue to guide and inspire the present and future generations of Greek-Americans in this country.

One

HOMELAND

Eastern Orthodox Christianity has shaped the culture and traditions of the people of Greece for nearly two millennia. In this photograph, a Greek Orthodox Priest stands in his vestments, wearing the *kalimavkion*, and holding a blessing cross. Standing next to him is his wife, the *presbytera*. They are flanked by their two children who, along with their mother, are wearing traditional ethnic clothing. (HKN.)

This color engraving from the late 1600s, possibly attributed to Venetian cartographer Vincenzo Coronelli or Flemish engraver Jacob Peeters, highlights the fortress of Monemvasia. Identified here are the old tower (A), the watchtower (B), the fortress gate (C), the fortress battery (D), the town (E), the gates of the village (F), the bridge broken by Venetians (G), and the fort made by Venetians to prevent relief efforts while laying siege to the Ottoman-controlled fortress (H). (HKN.)

Known as the Gibraltar of Greece and the Eastern Mediterranean, Monemvasia (or Malvasia, to the Venetians), is located in Lakonia province in the southern Peloponnesus. As the site of a powerful medieval fortress, Monemvasia had a strategic importance known throughout the Mediterranean. Founded in the early years of the Byzantine Empire, it was later ruled by the Pope, the Venetians, and the Ottomans before its eventual liberation in 1821. (HKN.)

The Church of the Panagia Hodegetria was built in the 12th century AD by Byzantine emperor Andronicus II. Located in the upper city, atop the rock of Monemvasia, it is the only church in the upper city to have survived Ottoman occupation intact, having been converted to a mosque to serve the Muslim population. It was later rededicated as the Church of Hagia Sophia. (HKN.)

Piraeus is the largest and most important port in Greece. This picture from the early 1960s highlights the newly consecrated Metropolitan Church of Agia Triada (Holy Trinity), which was destroyed during the allied bombardment of Piraeus in January 1944. In the background at left is a neoclassical building that houses the Naval Retirement Fund, which was founded in 1861 and is the oldest social security organization in Europe. (HKN.)

This 1971 postcard commemorating the 150th anniversary of Greek Independence depicts the Exodus from Missolonghi by Theodoros Vryzakis. Greek forces at Missolonghi had defeated Ottoman forces during two prior attempts by to take the city in 1822 and 1823. The heroic and tragic exodus from Missolonghi during the third siege of the city in 1826 led to the sacking of the city and the slaughter and enslavement of thousands. (HKN.)

This postcard depicts Capt. Frank Abney Hastings, a British naval officer and philhellene. Prior to arriving in Greece, Hastings had fought at the battle of Trafalgar during the Napoleonic wars and in the War of 1812. Under the command of Hastings, the *Kateria*, the first steam-powered warship in history, sailed for Greece in 1826. Wounded while trying to reclaim Missolonghi, Hastings died on Zakynthos on June 1, 1828. (HKN.)

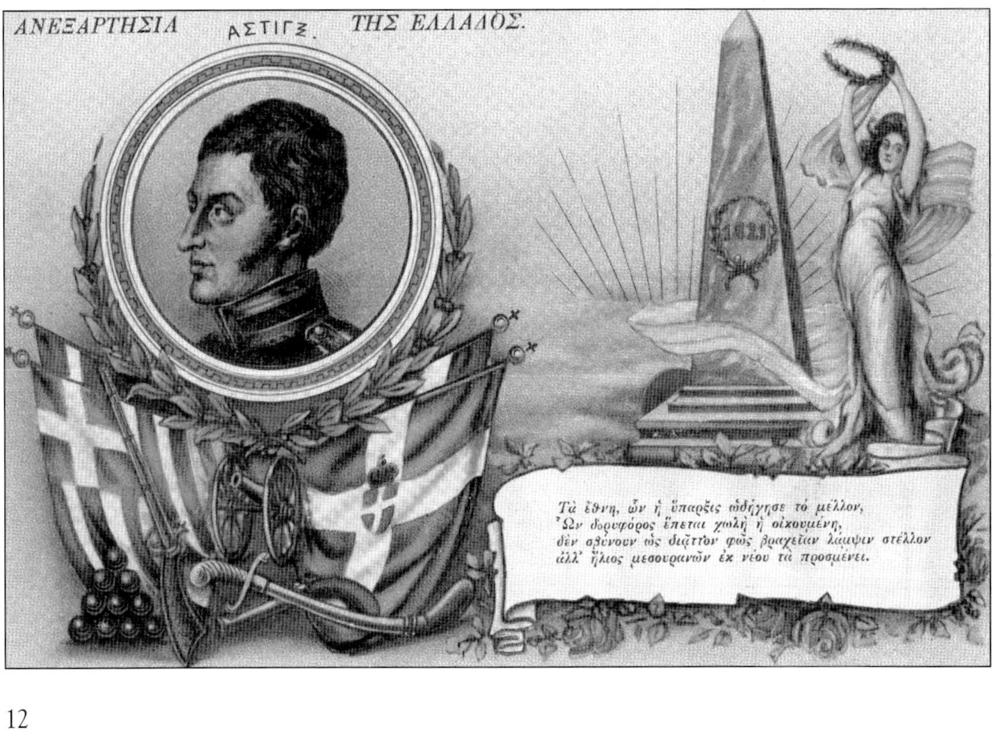

Evzones, or *Tsoliades*, are historically elite light infantry and mountain units of the Greek Army. Evzones derive their dress, specifically the *fustanella* (skirt/kilt), from the klephts. The klephts, or "thieves," were bandits turned militiamen who fought the Ottoman occupation from the mountains and rural areas of Greece. Today, evzones guard the Tomb of the Unknown Soldier in Syntagma Square in Athens and are members of the Presidential Guard. (HKN.)

Olga Constantinovna of Russia, a member of the Romanov dynasty, was 16 years old when she married King George I of Greece in St. Petersburg in 1867. As queen consort of Greece, she had eight children. King George I was assassinated in 1913, following the First Balkan War. Olga returned to Russia but eventually fled after the Russian Revolution. Queen dowager Olga returned to Greece as regent in 1920. (HKN.)

Georgios Averof was born in Metsovo, Epirus, and eventually moved to Alexandria, Egypt. A businessman and philanthropist, Averof gave millions of drachmas to fund educational, national, and military projects and institutions in Greece. Notably, Averof left 300,000 GBP to the Hellenic Navy in his will, which helped fund the construction of a Pisa-class armored cruiser, which was completed in 1910 and named in his honor; it served as the flagship of the Royal Hellenic Navy. (HKN.)

The genocide of Armenians, Assyrians, and Greeks by the Ottoman Empire led to the creation of the American Committee for Relief in the Near East (ACRNE) in 1915. ACRNE provided humanitarian aid and assistance to minority Christian populations fleeing persecution from the Ottoman Empire. Refugees were provided with food, clothing, services, education, agricultural training, and monetary loans. ACRNE saved hundreds of thousands of refugees and orphaned children. (Library of Congress.)

Nicholas Androutsopoulos (Andreson) is shown with his children in this photograph from the early 1900s. On his head, Nicholas wears a *fario*, a fez with a long tassel. He is also wearing a *fermeli*, or elaborate hand-embroidered woolen vest. Below that, he wears the traditional *fustanella*, a type of Greek kilt, along with *periskelides*, white woolen stockings, on his legs. Over his shoes, he wears *periknimides*, or spats. (WHM.)

In this family portrait of the Tsagarelis family from 1915, John T. Tsagarelis and Demetria Pappas Tsagarelis are surrounded by their children. In the middle of the photograph (between John and Demetria) is George Tsagarelis, who was born in 1899 in Pikerni, Arkadia, Greece. At the age of 16, George emigrated from Greece and arrived in Haverhill, where he lived for a few years before moving to Worcester in the early 1920s. (WHM.)

Vassil Panagiotou is pictured here around 1923 with his family, including his parents, Matthew and Konstantina Vozoris Panagiotou. Vassil was born in 1902 in Douviani (Dhuvjan), Argyrokastro (Gjirokastër), a Greek village in historic Northern Epirus, which is now within the modern borders of Albania. Vassil emigrated to the United States as a teenager in 1917, following his sister Alexandra and her husband, who had settled in Worcester a decade earlier. (WHM.)

Vassil Panagiotou married Zoitsa Economou in 1930. They are pictured with family in Douviani in this c. 1932 photograph. Vassil and Zoitsa had their first child, Dimitri, in 1931. Vassil returned to Worcester alone and brought Zoitsa and their infant son, Matthew, prior to the outbreak of World War II. Dimitri stayed with his grandparents in Douviani. Vassil, Zoitsa, and Matthew made Worcester their home. (WHM.)

Vassil and Zoitsa Panagiotou are shown in this c. 1930 image. Vassil bought a Howard Johnson's in West Boylston and renovated it, eventually selling it in 1970. Vassil and Zoitsa were active in the St. Spyridon community. Vassil was a member of AHEPA and a 32nd degree Mason. Their son Matthew was a dentist in Worcester and active in the community. Vassil passed away in 1984, and Zoitsa followed in 2009 at the age of 97. (WHM.)

This picture was taken in 1927 in Divri. In it are members of the Androutsopoulos (Andreson) family and others in their native village. The picture displays the clothing, dress, and styles of the time, especially the toothbrush mustache, which reached its peak popularity in the interwar years. Its later association with Nazi Germany's leader Adolf Hitler led to it becoming an unpopular and taboo style. (WHM.)

The development of state-issued identity documents was necessary for the bureaucratic functioning of the nation-state, including the governance, control, and surveillance of both citizens and noncitizens. More importantly, state-issued identity documents were integral for the development of nationalism and a cohesive national identity. Panagiotis Kasidakos was issued this identity card (*tautotita*) by the Hellenic Police of the Kingdom of Greece in Piraeus in 1948. (HKN.)

Paraskevi "Vicky" Helali (née Kasidakos) is shown in this mid-1960s photograph dressed as an evzone. Women and girls sometimes dress as evzones for cultural events and important holidays. The *fustanella* was declared the official court dress and national costume of Greece by King Otto in 1833. Since then, it has become synonymous with Greek identity, culture, and nationalism. Some claim the pleats number 400, representing the years of Ottoman occupation of Greece. (HKN.)

Grigoria Katelani (left), Panagiotis Nikolinakos (center), and Paraskevi Helali are pictured in Molaoi, Lakonia, around the mid-1960s. Born in Montreal, Canada, in 1963, Paraskevi grew up in Greece with her great-grandparents and extended family. Her parents, Panagiotis Kasidakos and Angeliki Kasidakos (née Nikolinakos), remained in Montreal, working multiple jobs. Their second child, George, was born in 1967. The Kasidakos family moved from Montreal to Worcester, Massachusetts, in 1970. (HKN.)

This photograph taken in Molaoi in the early 1960s shows Maria Katelani (née Nikolinakos) standing behind her parents, Panagiotis Nikolinakos and Konstantina Nikolinakos (née Krypotos). Standing between his grandparents is Panagiotis Nikolinakos, son of Nikolaos Nikolinakos and Despina Nikolinakos (née Hronopoulos). Panagiotis is holding Grigoria Katelani, daughter of Maria and Anastasios Katelani. The elder Panagiotis fought in Asia Minor as a Greek soldier during the Greco-Turkish War (1919–1922). (HKN.)

Panagiotis Kasidakos and an unidentified woman stand in front of the Parthenon atop the Athenian Acropolis in this photograph from the late 1950s. The Parthenon is the national symbol of Greece and one of the most important surviving buildings of Classical Greece. From antiquity to the present, the Parthenon has survived wars, fires, earthquakes, looting, and a catastrophic gunpowder explosion during the Morean or Sixth Ottoman-Venetian War. (HKN.)

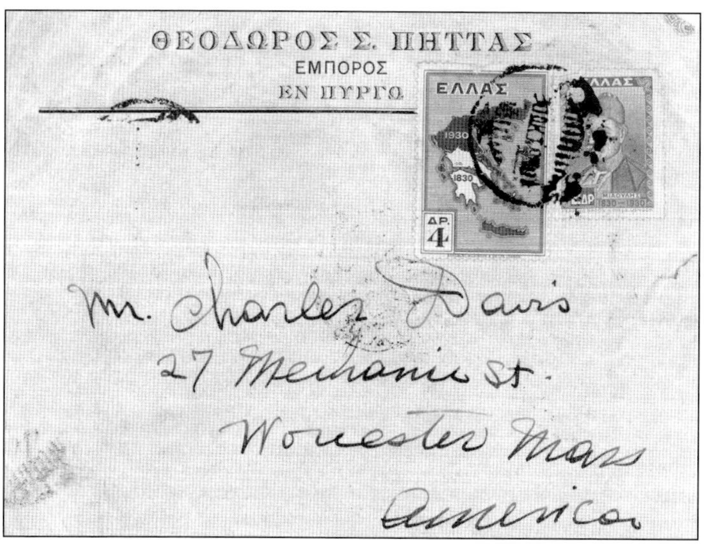

Prior to the advent of the internet, mail was the most important mode of communication between the diaspora and families, friends, and acquaintances who lived in Greece. Letters with the airmail etiquette "par avion" heralded joyous occasions and holiday greetings, as well as tragic news. This letter was sent to Charles Kotsilimbas Davis of Worcester from merchant Theodoros Pittas in Greece. (HKN.)

Two

IMMIGRATION

This photograph from the mid- to late 1800s shows a Greek man posing in his traditional clothing, including the *fustanella*, *fario*, vest, stockings, and spats. This photograph was taken by pioneering photographer James Wallace "J.W." Black at his studio at 173 Washington Street in Boston, Massachusetts. Black's prolific output included pictures of Walt Whitman, Union and Confederate Civil War soldiers, prominent women, and formerly enslaved people. (HKN.)

Evanthia Koutoulas (née Efthimiou) arrived by boat to the United States around 1953 or 1954. She was born in Douviani, Northern Epirus, to Thomas and Olga Efthimiou (née Tsitsos). She married Jason D. Koutoulas, and they co-owned and operated Jason's Pizza in Worcester for decades. She served as president of the Ladies Philoptochos Society at St. Spyridon and was active in the church, the seniors' group, and the Epirotic Society. (WHM.)

Persefony Capsalis (née Venetis) was born in Northern Epirus to George and Katina Venetis (née Kitsakis). While Greeks in Northern Epirus fought for their autonomy and created the Autonomous Republic of Northern Epirus in 1914, political instability in Greece and the eventual defeat of Greek forces in the Asia Minor Catastrophe forced Greece to cede Northern Epirus to Albania in 1921. Persefony's passport shown here was issued by Albania. (WHM.)

2

SHENIMET E TITULLARIT
SIGNALEMENT DU TITULAIRE

Shtati: / Taille: 1.65
Mosha: / Age: 1912
Balli: / Front: Regulier
Sytë: / Yeux: Chatanies
Hunda: / Nez: Regulier
Goja: / Bouche: Tolem
Flokët: / Cheveux: chatanies
Mjekra: / Barbe: aucun
Musteqet: / Moustaches: aucun
Ngjyra: / Teint: Brunes
Shenja të veçanta: / Signes particuliers: aucun

3

Pasaporta për ku lëshohet: / Destination: Për Amerikë Pour U.S.A. Për një mot
Për sa asht e vleftshme: / Valable: Pour un an
Qëllimi i udhtimit: / But du voyage: Tran Buit Laj

MBRETNIA SHQIPTARE
Fr. 10
TAKSË PASAPORTASH
20 QINDAR 20

8/2/34

Nënshkrimi i kryetarit të zyrës / Signature du chef de Bureau

NËNPREFEKTURA LIBOHOVË

Taksë monopoli

"ITALIA"
SEDE SUCCURSALE DI NAPOLI
P.fo CONTE DI SAVOIA
Data di partenza 6 MAR 1934
SECONDA CLASSE ECONOMICA
Il Signor PERSIFONIS CAPSALIS e figli
ha espletato le operazioni sanitari.
IL MEDICO DELLA COMPAGN
TIP ESPERIA - NAPOLI

Persefony Capsalis emigrated with her children to Milford, Massachusetts. This is the second-class ticket for her transatlantic journey; she departed on March 6, 1934, on the SS *Conte di Savoia*, or "Count of Savoy," an Italian ocean liner that was completed two years earlier. The *Conte di Savoia* had three of the largest (at the time) anti-rolling gyroscopes built into it—they ultimately failed to work effectively. (WHM.)

THE UNITED STATES OF AMERICA
ORIGINAL
TO BE GIVEN TO
THE PERSON NATURALIZED
No. 8034380
CERTIFICATE OF NATURALIZATION
Petition No. 51385
Personal description of holder as of date of naturalization: Date of birth March 28, 1912 sex female
complexion medium color of eyes hazel color of hair brown-grey height 5 feet 5 inches;
weight 165 pounds; visible distinctive marks none
Marital status married former nationality Albanian
I certify that the description above given is true, and that the photograph affixed hereto is a likeness of me.
Persefony Capsalis
(Complete and true signature of holder)
Commonwealth of Massachusetts } ss:
County of Worcester
Be it known, that at a term of the Superior Court of Massachusetts
held pursuant to law at Worcester, Massachusetts
on June 22, 1960 the Court having found that
PERSEFONY CAPSALIS
then residing at 31 Blossom Street, Worcester, Massachusetts
intends to reside permanently in the United States (when so required by the Naturalization Laws of the United States), had in all other respects complied with the applicable provisions of such naturalization laws, and was entitled to be admitted to citizenship, thereupon ordered that such person be and (s)he was admitted as a citizen of the United States of America.
In testimony whereof the seal of the court is hereunto affixed this 22nd
day of June in the year of our Lord nineteen hundred and sixty and of our Independence the one hundred and eighty-fourth.
James J. Joyce
Clerk of the Superior Court.
By Deputy Clerk.
It is a violation of the U.S. Code (and punishable as such) to copy, print, photograph, or otherwise illegally use this certificate.
DEPARTMENT OF JUSTICE

Persefony became a naturalized US citizen on June 22, 1960. Her former nationality is listed as Albanian due to the aforementioned status of Northern Epirus. She was married to Vassilios Capsalis, and they had three children. She worked for Table Talk Pies and then for Westboro State Hospital, from which she retired in 1974. Persefony was active in the church, the seniors' group, and the Ladies Philoptochos Society. (WHM.)

THE UNITED STATES OF AMERICA

ORIGINAL
TO BE GIVEN TO
THE PERSON NATURALIZED

No. 5374499

CERTIFICATE OF NATURALIZATION

Petition No. 34119

Personal description of holder as of date of naturalization: Age 45 years; sex female; color white; complexion medium; color of eyes hazel; color of hair dk. brown; height 5 feet 6 inches; weight 175 pounds; visible distinctive marks none
Marital status married; former nationality Turkish
I certify that the description above given is true, and that the photograph affixed hereto is a likeness of me.

catina Peepas
(Complete and true signature of holder)

Commonwealth of Massachusetts } ss:
County of Worcester }

Be it known, that at a term of the Superior Court of Massachusetts held pursuant to law at Worcester, Massachusetys on Jan. 9, 1942 the Court having found that Catina Peepas then residing at 640 Grafton Street, Worcester, Mass. intends to reside permanently in the United States (when so required by the Naturalization Laws of the United States), had in all other respects complied with the applicable provisions of such naturalization laws, and was entitled to be admitted to citizenship, thereupon ordered that such person be and (s)he was admitted as a citizen of the United States of America.
In testimony whereof the seal of the court is hereunto affixed this 9th day of January in the year of our Lord nineteen hundred and forty-two and of our Independence the one hundred and sixty-sixth

Seal

William C. Bowen
Clerk of the Superior Court.
By [signature] Deputy Clerk.

It is a violation of the U.S. Code (and punishable as such) to copy, print, photograph, or otherwise illegally use this certificate.

DEPARTMENT OF JUSTICE

This is the naturalization certificate of Catina (Aikaterini) Peepas (née Mellas). In June 1913, Catina arrived around in the United States from Aretsou (Darıca), Turkey, via Patras, Greece, on the SS *Oceania*, a ship of the Austro-American Line. Aretsou, located near Constantinople, was a predominantly Greek town. Following the Asia Minor Catastrophe, Greeks were forced to leave Aretsou as a result of the exchange of populations stipulated in the 1923 Treaty of Lausanne. (WHM.)

2

ΧΑΡΑΚΤΗΡΙΣΤΙΚΑ
SIGNALEMENTS

Συζύγου — Femme

Ἐπάγγελμα / Profession: ΟΙΚΙΑΚΑ / SANS PROFESSION
Τόπος καὶ χρόνος γεννήσεως / Lieu et date de naissance: Μολάοι 1932
Διαμονὴ / Domicile
Πρόσωπον / Visage: ΚΑΝΟΝΙΚΟΝ / RÉGULIER
Χρῶμα ὀφθαλμῶν / Couleur des yeux
Χρῶμα κόμης / Couleur des cheveux: ΚΑΣΤΑΝΑ / CHATAINS
Ἰδιαίτερα σημεῖα / Signes particuliers

ΤΕΚΝΑ — ENFANTS
Ὄνομα / Nom | Ἡλικία / Age | Γένος / Sexe

3

Συζύγου — Femme
Φωτογραφία / Photo

Ὑπογραφὴ κατόχου / Signature du titulaire
καὶ τῆς συζύγου / et de sa femme

ΥΠΟΓΡΑΦΗ ΤΟΥ ΧΟΡΗΓΗΣΑΝΤΟΣ ΤΟ ΔΙΑΒΑΤΗΡΙΟΝ ΥΠΑΛΛΗΛΟΥ:
SIGNATURE DE L'AGENT DÉLIVRANT LE PASSEPORT:
LE CHEF DE LA SECTION DES PASSEPORTS AU MINISTÈRE DE L'INTÉRIEUR

These are pages of a Greek passport belonging to Angeliki Kasidakos, who was born in Molaoi, Lakonia, in 1932. Following the Greek Civil War, Kasidakos—a young and single woman—embarked on the long journey to Canada in search of work, safety, and a better life. This passport was issued by the Kingdom of Greece in the 1950s. Her profession is listed as *oikiaka*, or "housework." (HKN.)

Above, Panagiotis Kasidakos (wearing a dark suit and dark glasses with a cigarette in hand) is shown aboard the SS *Queen Frederica* on a transatlantic crossing in the 1960s. Seated to his right is Mary Kourkoulis (née Speridakos), the sister of Athanasios Speridakos. Below, Kasidakos (far left) leads the men in a traditional Greek dance on the *Queen Frederica*. The journey from Greece to the United States—via ports of call that could include Canada, Italy, Gibraltar, and Spain—took over a week to complete. Built as the SS *Malolo* in 1927, this vessel was transferred to the National Hellenic American Line and renamed the *Queen Frederica* in 1954. The *Queen Frederica* provided passengers with grand dinners and entertainment, including music, shows, and dancing. Both of these pictures were taken by Nicos Gounarakis. (Both, HKN.)

THE UNITED STATES OF AMERICA

No. 10476249

CERTIFICATE OF NATURALIZATION

Petition No. 57134

Alien Registration No. 30 737 479

·ORIGINAL·

Personal description of holder as of date of naturalization: Date of birth March 5, 1926 sex Male complexion Medium color of eyes Brown color of hair Brown height 5 feet 11 inches; weight 185 pounds; visible distinctive marks Scar on left wrist Marital status Married Country of former nationality Canada

I certify that the description above given is true, and that the photograph affixed hereto is a likeness of me.

Panagiotis Kasidakos
(Complete and true signature of holder)

Commonwealth of Massachusetts
County of Worcester ss:

Be it known that at a term of the Superior Court of Massachusetts held pursuant to law at Worcester, Massachusetts on March 3, 1976 the Court having found that PANAGIOTIS KASIDAKOS then residing at 1 Federal Place, Worcester, Massachusetts intends to reside permanently in the United States (when so required by the Naturalization Laws of the United States), had in all other respects complied with the applicable provisions of such naturalization laws, and was entitled to be admitted to citizenship, thereupon ordered that such person be and (s)he was admitted as a citizen of the United States of America.

In testimony whereof the seal of the court is hereunto affixed this 3rd day of March in the year of our Lord nineteen hundred and seventy-six

Seal

James J. Joyce
Clerk of the Superior Court.
By Deputy Clerk.

IT IS PUNISHABLE BY U. S. LAW TO COPY, PRINT OR PHOTOGRAPH THIS CERTIFICATE.

DEPARTMENT OF JUSTICE

Above is the naturalization certificate of Panagiotis Kasidakos. Born on March 5, 1926, in Sykia, Lakonia, he eventually moved to Worcester via Montreal, Canada, where he also gained citizenship. This certificate issued in 1976 is especially unique, as its background image features the logo commissioned by the American Revolution Bicentennial Commission, which says, "American Revolution Bicentennial: 1776–1976." Below is the naturalization certificate of Angeliki Kasidakos, wife of Panagiotis. Angeliki became a naturalized US citizen on December 11, 2000. Angeliki had also become a Canadian citizen and was not required to renounce that. Thus, Angeliki and Panagiotis were triple citizens of Greece, Canada, and the United States. (Both, HKN.)

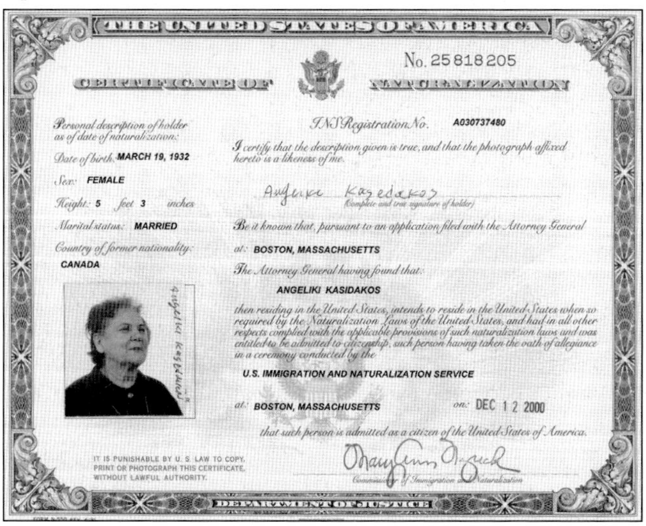
THE UNITED STATES OF AMERICA

No. 25818205

CERTIFICATE OF NATURALIZATION

Personal description of holder as of date of naturalization:

Date of birth: MARCH 19, 1932

Sex: FEMALE

Height: 5 feet 3 inches

Marital status: MARRIED

Country of former nationality: CANADA

INS Registration No. A030737480

I certify that the description given is true, and that the photograph affixed hereto is a likeness of me.

(Complete and true signature of holder)

Be it known that, pursuant to an application filed with the Attorney General at: BOSTON, MASSACHUSETTS

The Attorney General having found that: ANGELIKI KASIDAKOS

then residing in the United States, intends to reside in the United States when so required by the Naturalization Laws of the United States, and had in all other respects complied with the applicable provisions of such naturalization laws and was entitled to be admitted to citizenship, such person having taken the oath of allegiance in a ceremony conducted by the

U.S. IMMIGRATION AND NATURALIZATION SERVICE

at: BOSTON, MASSACHUSETTS on: DEC 12 2000

that such person is admitted as a citizen of the United States of America.

Commissioner of Immigration and Naturalization

IT IS PUNISHABLE BY U. S. LAW TO COPY, PRINT OR PHOTOGRAPH THIS CERTIFICATE WITHOUT LAWFUL AUTHORITY.

DEPARTMENT OF JUSTICE

Three

FAMILY

On August 4, 1952, Vasilios Economou and Evrydiki Garoulis were married at St. Spyridon Greek Orthodox Church. In this photograph, construction at St. Spyridon is incomplete. Vasilios was born to Constantine and Olga Economou (née Panagiotou) in Douviani, Northern Epirus. Evrydiki was born to Vasilios and Agathi Evrydiki (née Andoni) in Athens, Greece. Olga Economou sold Panagiotis Kasidakos the three-decker home at 1 Federal Place in 1972. (WHM.)

George T. and Catina Peepas (née Mellas) posed for this professional photograph in 1914. George was born on May 10, 1887, in Constantinople, Ottoman Empire. He left Constantinople at age 22 and arrived at Ellis Island via Piraeus, Greece, in 1910. George was a tailor and opened his first shop at 149 Mechanic Street. This picture shows the prevailing fashions of the time, including George's bowler hat. (WHM.)

George T. and Catina Peepas sat for this professional picture in 1914. While the above photograph shows them wearing hats and coats, they are more relaxed here, posing for the photographer while seated. George wears a lounge suit—a three-piece suit of the time period. Catina wears a long dress with jewelry. Note the hairstyles, which are reflective of the era. (WHM.)

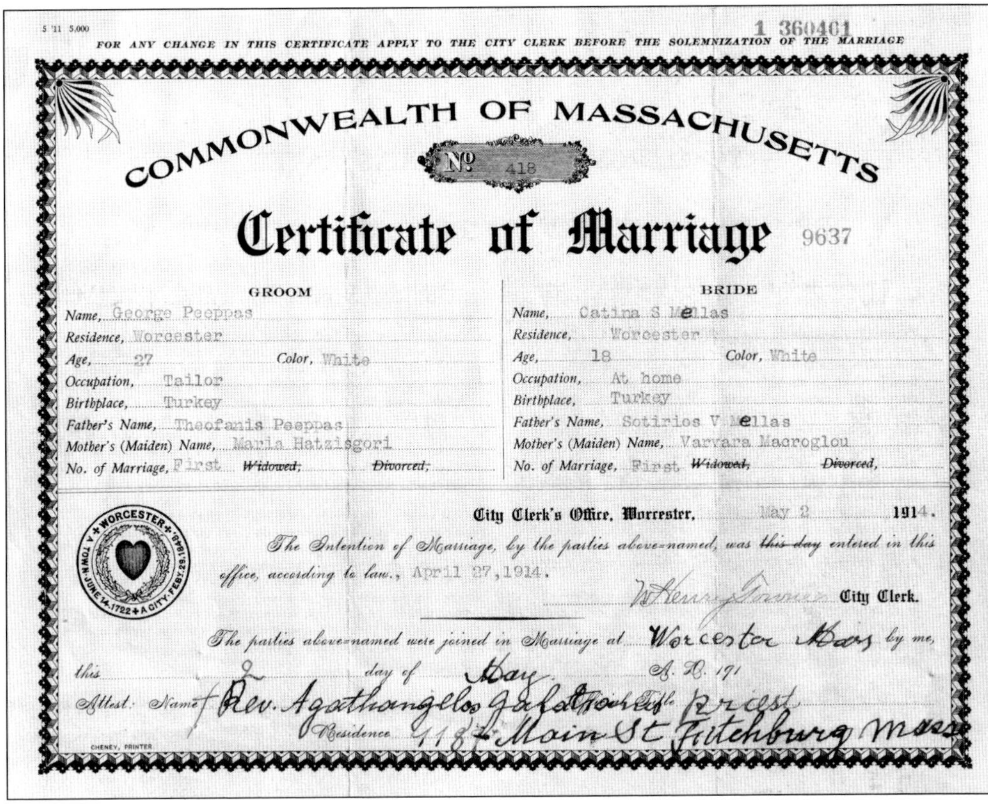

5 '11 5,000 1 360401

FOR ANY CHANGE IN THIS CERTIFICATE APPLY TO THE CITY CLERK BEFORE THE SOLEMNIZATION OF THE MARRIAGE

COMMONWEALTH OF MASSACHUSETTS

Nº 418

Certificate of Marriage 9637

GROOM		BRIDE	
Name,	George Peepas	Name,	Catina S Mellas
Residence,	Worcester	Residence,	Worcester
Age,	27 Color, White	Age,	18 Color, White
Occupation,	Tailor	Occupation,	At home
Birthplace,	Turkey	Birthplace,	Turkey
Father's Name,	Theofanis Peepas	Father's Name,	Sotirios V Mellas
Mother's (Maiden) Name,	Maria Hatzisgori	Mother's (Maiden) Name,	Varvara Macroglou
No. of Marriage,	First ~~Widowed,~~ ~~Divorced,~~	No. of Marriage,	First ~~Widowed,~~ ~~Divorced,~~

City Clerk's Office, Worcester, May 2 1914.

The Intention of Marriage, by the parties above-named, was ~~this day~~ entered in this office, according to law., April 27,1914.

W Henry Towne City Clerk.

The parties above-named were joined in Marriage at Worcester Mass by me, this 2 day of May A. D. 191

Attest: Name Rev. Agathangelos Galatianos Title priest

Residence 118 Main St Fitchburg Mass

CHENEY, PRINTER

George Peepas married Catina S. Mellas on May 2, 1914, in Worcester. The Greek-born Agathangelos Galatianos (spelled "Galateanos" on the 1920 US census paperwork) of Fitchburg, Massachusetts, officiated. In 1919, Reverend Agathangelos was a priest at the Greek Orthodox Church in Mason City, Iowa. According to George and Catina's granddaughters Betsy T. Liangas (née Peepas) and Katherine T. Peepas, this was one of the first Greek weddings in Worcester. (WHM.)

George and Catina Peepas posed for their wedding portrait in 1914. Catina wears a distinctive wedding dress reminiscent of Victorian fashion, with long white gloves that extend to the elbows and a covered neck. George's suit has a high-starched white collar with only a thin opening for a tie. Fashion was influenced by trends in Europe, especially in France and Britain. (WHM.)

George (seated) and Catina Peepas are pictured here with their son Theofanis G. in 1929. Theofanis was born in 1915. He attended Rice Square Elementary School, Grafton Street Junior High School, and Commerce High School. He was active in the community, serving on the parish council of St. Spyridon Greek Orthodox Church, and was a founding member of the St. Spyridon Greek School Alumni Association. (WHM.)

George and Catherine Tsagarelis (née Angelopoulos) are shown here. George was a prominent and beloved leader in Worcester's Greek community. A philanthropist, he served St. Spyridon Greek Orthodox Church in various positions over the years. He was a member of the Order of AHEPA for 40 years, an Archon of the Ecumenical Patriarchate, a trustee of Hellenic College Holy Cross Greek Orthodox School of Theology, and a member of the Archdiocesan Council. (WHM.)

The Moschos family celebrated the 50th wedding anniversary of Constantine M. Moschos and Vasiliky Strates in 1978. Constantine was born in 1900 in the village of Phiniki, Epirus. Vasiliky was born in 1909 to Christos and Eleni Strates in Constantinople. Christos and Vasiliky married on November 4, 1928, in Phiniki. Vasiliky graduated from the Scottish College in Constantinople. She later worked for the British Bank in Constantinople. (WHM.)

From left to right are (first row, seated) Despina "Tina" J. Leasca (née Rougas), Despina Tsiotras, Kay Chopas (née Rougas), and Helen Rougas (née Drapos); (second row, standing) Peter G. Leasca, Angeliki Kasidakos, Panagiotis Kasidakos, George Chopas, and Peter J. Rougas. Peter, Despina, and Kay were children of John and Calliope (Stappas) Rougas. Calliope was the sister of Paraskevi Kasdiakos (née Stappas), the mother of Panagiotis. (HKN.)

Pictured above from left to right are (first row) Kalliopi Kasidakos (née Bardis) with infant Leonidas Kasidakos, Despina Tsiotras (née Kasidakos) with infant Emmanuel Tsiotras, Paraskevi Kasidakos (née Stappas), Leonidas Speridakos (seated on the floor), Leonidas Kasidakos, Stavroula Speridakos (née Kasidakos) with daughter Constantina Kapeleris (née Speridakos) standing in front of her, and Eleni Kasidakos (née Alexandrou) with infant Leonidas Kasidakos; (second row, standing) Panagiotis Speridakos, Konstantinos Kassidakos, Panagiotis Tsiotras, Panagiotis Kasidakos, Athanasios Speridakos, Nikolaos Kasidakos. The picture of Panagiotis and Angeliki Kasidakos at left was taken in Montreal, Canada, in the early 1960s. Panagiotis left Greece on October 26, 1960, to meet his fiancée, Angeliki, who had arrived in Montreal four years earlier. Their marriage was arranged—the result of a friendship between their mothers. Their correspondence had included pictures of themselves. They married two weeks after Panagiotis arrived in Montreal. (Both, HKN.)

The photograph at right of Panagiotis and Angeliki Kasidakos was taken in Montreal, Canada, in the early 1960s. Angeliki and Panagiotis became Canadian citizens and later—after being sponsored by Peter Leasca to come to the United States—moved their family to Worcester, Massachusetts, in 1970. Their new life afforded them opportunities they would have been unable to achieve in Greece due to political repression following the Greek Civil War. Panagiotis and Angeliki were married on November 13, 1960, at the Holy Trinity Greek Orthodox Church at 8 Sherbrooke Street W. in Montreal, Canada. Below, from left to right are Despina Maintanis (née Dounetos), Kyriakos Petrakos, Julia Karahalios, Kay Chopas, an unidentified child, Calliope Rougas (née Stappas), Panagiotis and Angeliki, Arhonto Dounetos (née Stappas), Angelo Maintanis, Marion Centracchio, Nikolaos Nikolinakos, Albert Centracchio, Mary Centracchio (née Dounetos), and John Dounetos. (Both, HKN.)

Paraskevi (née Stappas) and Leonidas Kasidakos (right) drink Greek coffee with pictures of Panagiotis and Angeliki Kasidakos in a photograph taken in Greece. This image was sent to Panagiotis and Angeliki in Montreal. Before the advent of video calls, it was common for people to pose with pictures of family in the diaspora that would be sent abroad. This loving gesture could help faraway friends and family feel emotionally close despite the physical separation. (HKN.)

The Kasidakos family poses next to their three-decker at 1 Federal Place near Elm Park in the late 1970s. In the background are Blessed Sacrament Church, a Roman Catholic church, and Newton Hill. From left to right are George P. Kasidakos, Tina Kassidakos, Panagiotis Kasidakos, Angeliki Kasidakos, Paraskevi Helali (née Kasidakos), and Emmanuel K. Kassidakos. Emmanuel is the son of Konstantinos Kassidakos, the brother of Panagiotis. (HKN.)

Family gathered at the home of Panagiotis and Angeliki Kasidakos at 1 Federal Place in the 1980s. Standing is Konstantinos Kassidakos. Seated from left to right are Despina "Tina" J. Leasca (née Rougas), Nikolaos Kasidakos, Calliope Rougas (Stappas), and Panagiotis Kasidakos. Nikolaos fought against fascist Italy in Northern Greece; later, as a member of EAM-ELAS, he fought against Nazi Germany forces in Greece. (HKN.)

From left to right are Nikolaos Kasidakos, Peter J. Rougas, and Helen Rougas (née Drapos) at the house of Panagiotis and Angeliki Kasidakos. Walking through the doorway is Athanasios Speridakos, and reflected in the mirror is Joanne Bilzerian (née Leasca). Nikolaos, Panagiotis, and Konstantinos Kassidakos were first cousins of Peter Rougas, Despina Leasca, and Kay Chopas. For Greeks, family gatherings and celebrations are common, especially around religious rituals, rites, and holidays. (HKN.)

These photographs were taken by Olan Mills at St. Spyridon Greek Orthodox Cathedral in 1996. Pictured above are, from left to right, (first row, standing) Christopher and Peter Helali; (second row, seated) Panagiotis and Angeliki Kasidakos; (third row, standing) Davood "David" Helali, George Kasidakos, and Paraskevi Helali. As a tailor, Panagiotis had a classic and elegant taste in men's and women's fashion. Panagiotis strove to dress his family impeccably well. Pictured below are Panagiotis (left), Angeliki (center), and George Kasidakos. These pictures were taken for a church directory that included portraits of families and parishioners of St. Spyridon. (Both, HKN.)

Four

Culture, Tradition, and Religion

Sunday school students pose for a photograph on the steps of St. Spyridon Greek Orthodox Church on Orange Street in the early 1940s. Rev. Demetrios Makris is pictured to the right at the top of the stairs; he was appointed as the priest in September 1940 and served in that capacity until he resigned in September 1944 to teach theology as a professor at the Greek Orthodox seminary. (WHM.)

This 1924 photograph shows the cornerstone-laying ceremony for St. Spyridon Greek Orthodox Church on Orange Street. A crane is holding a large stone at left. The contractor that built the church was Ernest Whitehead and Company. The construction of the church cost approximately $65,000, with $30,000 held in a mortgage. (WHM.)

A priest conducts the sacrament of baptism at St. Spyridon Greek Orthodox Church on Orange Street. The icons in the background are not Byzantine in style but Western; they are sometimes referred to as Italianate. This was a common feature of Orthodox churches in Greece and the West starting in the 19th century and lasting through the mid-20th century. There was later a revival of Byzantine iconography. (WHM.)

The first St. Spyridon Greek Orthodox Church was located on Orange Street in Worcester. This was the first church built by Worcester's Greek community. It was designed by Armenian architect Hachadoor Sarkis Demoorjian and completed in 1925. This church is similar to Demoorjian's other church project, the Greek Orthodox Cathedral of New England (later renamed the Annunciation Greek Orthodox Cathedral) in Boston. Both are classical revival churches with Byzantine modifications. (HKN.)

This picture was taken by George Cocaine in the narthex of St. Spyridon Greek Orthodox Church on Orange Street. Archbishop Michael of North and South America is wearing his *mandyas* and holding his *paterissa*. Rev. Athanasios Rizos is holding the Gospel, and Rev. Demetrios T. Makris is to his left. (WHM.)

The choir of St. Spyridon is shown here in the early 1950s. Rev. Athanasios Rizos is on the right. To his left is Loukia S. Bitzas (née Sarando). Bitzas was the first full-time choir director and served in that capacity from November 1946 until June 1953, when her sister, Elpida S. Milias (née Sarando) took over. Milias was choir director for over 50 years, retiring in 2006. (WHM.)

Choir members posed for this photograph dated 1949. Rev. Athanasios Rizos is third from the left in the first row. Loukia S. Bitzas (née Sarando), the St. Spyridon choir director, is at farthest right in the front row. To the left of Loukia is her husband, Rev. Thomas G. Bitzas, who passed away in 1955. (WHM.)

This photograph by George Cocaine shows an unidentified bishop (left), an unidentified young girl, and James A. Gourgouras (right), a reporter for the *Telegram & Gazette*. In the early years of the Greek community in Worcester, bishops from around the United States and Greece would travel to visit the community, including bishops from areas in Greece and Northern Epirus that had strong ties to the Worcester community. (WHM.)

From left to right are Peter L. Bell (Panagiotis Beloyiannis), John Kotsilimbas Davis, James A. Gourgouras, an unidentified bishop, George Andreson, and Charles Kotsilimbas Davis. This photograph was taken by George Cocaine. Bell was born in Hudson, Massachusetts, to Leonidas Beloyiannis and Christina Beloyiannis (née Papasyriopoulos), who came from Tsipiana and Divry, Greece. (WHM.)

The youth of St. Spyridon perform various skits during the celebrations commemorating the start of the Greek War of Independence on March 25, 1821. In this photograph taken by George Cocaine, children are dressed as evzones, Ottoman soldiers, women in traditional dresses, and military officials. (WHM.)

Dressed as a soldier, a girl (left) places a crown on the girl to her left, who likely symbolizes Lady Liberty or the personification of Greece as a woman as painted by Theodoros Vryzakis in *Grateful Hellas* (1858). Boys dressed as evzones, a sailor, and a Boy Scout salute her. Below them is a boy dressed as an Orientalized depiction of an Ottoman Turk. This photograph was taken by George Cocaine. (WHM.)

Dressed as an evzone, a boy with a BB gun in hand poses for a photograph next to a girl in traditional dress. The boy has a fake mustache similar to the depictions of kelphts in the Greek War of Independence. On the boy's head, the *fario* has a crown emblem, denoting the monarchy of Greece. This picture was taken by George Cocaine. (WHM.)

Greek school students gathered to celebrate the March 25 holiday in this c. 1980 image. In the back (at center) is Nikolaos Tzoumbas, the principal of the St. Spyridon Greek School. Nikolaos was born in Douviani, Greece, to Leonidas and Efthalia Tzoumbas (née Kyriakos). During World War II, he was captured by the Italian army and sent to the Dachau concentration camp in Nazi Germany, where he remained until its liberation in 1945. (HKN.)

Paraskevi Helali (née Kasidakos) posed for this professional photograph at Loring Studio, which was located at 564 Main Street in Worcester. She wears a traditional Greek dress that was specifically made to be worn for Greek national holidays as well as various cultural events, Greek school recitations, and dances. (HKN.)

Paraskevi Helali poses for a photograph wearing a historic Greek dress belonging to Aphrodite Tsouros (née Litos). The ceremonial Greek gown was a wedding dress made by the father of her husband, John Tsouros. It is very elaborate, sewn with real gold thread, and has a gold belt with coins. Aphrodite was a past president of St. Spyridon's Philoptochos Society. The dress was later donated to the Worcester Historical Museum. (HKN.)

Young women of the Greek dance group at St. Spyridon Greek Orthodox Church in Worcester are shown here in 1973. Some of the women are dressed as evzones, wearing the *fustanella*, while others wear traditional clothing from different regions in Greece. From left to right are Maria Singas, Eleni Palaskas, Donna Panagiotou, Ann Mello, Martha Panagiotou, Katina Venetis, Mary Koumanelis, Maria Shocas, and Marilyn Mello. (WHM.)

Students from the afternoon Greek school program at St. Spyridon are dressed up for their graduation in 1977. From left to right are Sophia Tatsis, Linda Cocavessis, Elizabeth Baker, and Maria Vasiliadis (née Koutoulas). The Greek school was essential to continuing the Greek language, culture, and traditions in the United States. (WHM.)

Children of St. Spyridon Greek Orthodox Church Sunday school stood on the front steps of the church near the intersection of Russell and Elm Streets for this picture in the 1950s. The church's Sunday school was and continues to be critical to nurturing and educating young people about the Orthodox Christian faith and traditions. (WHM.)

Children of St. Spyridon Greek Orthodox Church Sunday school stand on the steps leading to the sanctuary inside the church in this 1970s picture. Rev. George Stephanides is in the center of the back row. St. Spyridon started its Sunday school programs in the 1920s. (HKN.)

The altar boys of St. Spyridon Greek Orthodox Church are shown in this c. 1953 photograph. Pictured from left to right are (first row) Yiorgos Tsifrikas, Eleftherios Kontaxis, Demetrios Pialtos, Nikolaos Anastasiou, Pantelis Tsanis, and Konstantinos Stathis; (second row) Sotirios Zoulas, Demetrios Xristofidis, Spyridon Kommitas, Demetrios Tzias, Demetrios Economou, Leonidas Biliouris, and Ioannis Rizos; (third row) Nikolaos Gatzoyiannis, Pavlos Manos, Rev. Athanasios Rizos, Simeon Gourousis, and Spyros Kapsalis. (WHM.)

Many seminarians from Holy Cross Greek Orthodox School of Theology in Brookline, Massachusetts, have done practicums and training at St. Spyridon in Worcester. They have opportunities to help at the altar and chant. This photograph shows some young seminarians with Rev. Dean Paleologos (in the center of the second row) and Rev. Nicholas K. Apostola (standing to the right of Reverend Paleologos). (WHM.)

Archbishop Iakovos performs the sacrament of ordination at St. Spyridon Greek Orthodox Church. The unidentified deacon is preparing for the priesthood with two priests to help guide and bless him. The priests are holding the deacon's arms. Rev. Athanasios Rizos is to the deacon's left. This photograph was taken by George Cocaine. (WHM.)

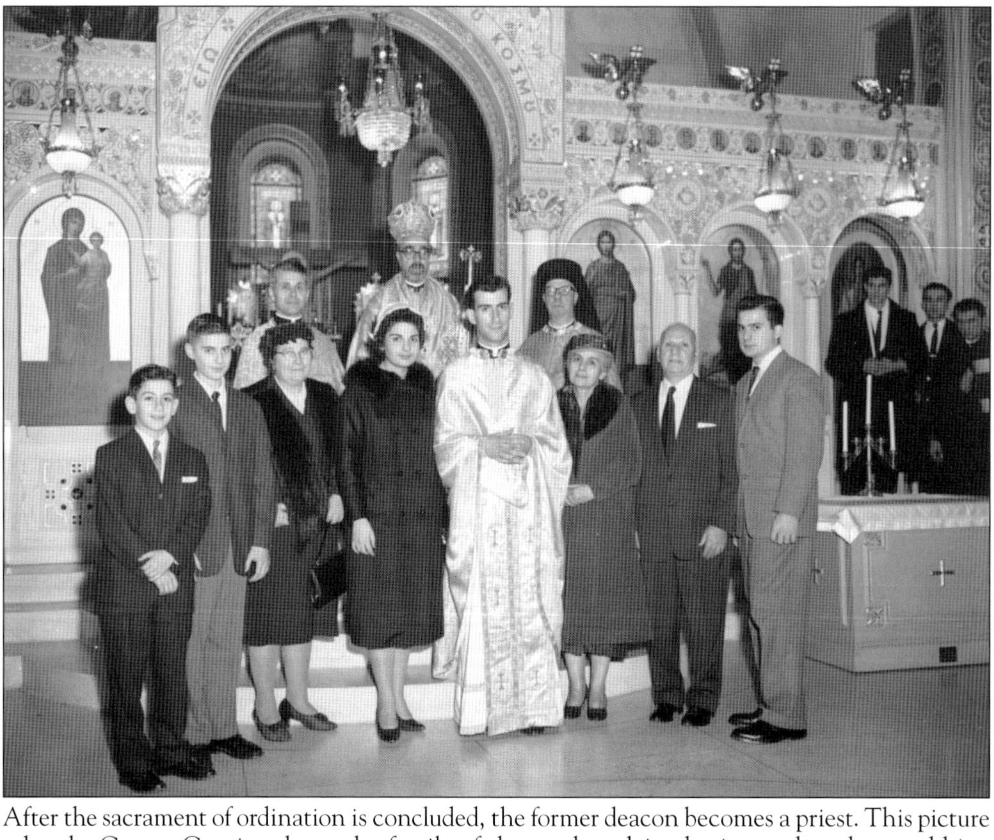

After the sacrament of ordination is concluded, the former deacon becomes a priest. This picture taken by George Cocaine shows the family of the newly ordained priest gathered around him. Behind them, at the top of the stairs leading to the sanctuary, is Archbishop Iakovos. To the right of Archbishop Iakovos is Rev. Athanasios Rizos. (WHM.)

The hierarchs, clergy, and lay leaders of St. Spyridon Greek Orthodox Church gathered for this 1950s photograph. From left to right are (first row, seated) Bishop Iakovos of Apameia, Archbishop Michael of North and South America, and an unidentified bishop; (second row, standing) unidentified, Rev. Athanasios Rizos, Angelus Cotsidas, George Tsagarelis, Theodore Tonna, unidentified, Rev. Solon Tsandikos, and Charles Kotsilimbas Davis. (WHM.)

George Tsagarelis (second from right), who was well known for his generosity, philanthropy, and dedication to St. Spyridon Greek Orthodox Church, was awarded the Man of the Year Award by the Ladies Philoptochos Society of St. Spyridon in 1961. Tsagarelis had served as president of the parish council in 1945 and again from 1950 to 1954. (WHM.)

From left to right, Archbishop Michael of North and South America is joined by Rev. Solon Tsandikos, George Tsagarelis, and James Andreson in a photograph taken in the 1960s. The importance of the Greek community of Worcester is apparent in the frequent visitation by hierarchs of the church. (WHM.)

George Tsagarelis (far left) is presenting a bishop's miter to Bishop Demetrios T. Makris of Olympus. Rev. Athanasios Rizos stands to the left of Bishop Demetrios. According to some scholars, Orthodox bishops started to wear miters following the fall of Constantinople in 1453. Scholars also hypothesize that the miter was modeled after the imperial crown of the Byzantine emperors. (WHM.)

Bishop Demetrios T. Makris (left) of Olympus is handing a sliced piece of *vasilopita* (New Year's Day bread) to George Tsagarelis. This is often done as a fundraiser for the community or various causes as needed. *Vasilopita* is translated as Basil's pita—a reference to St. Basil, whose feast day falls on January 1. (WHM.)

Rev. Solon Tsandikos joined area Orthodox clergy for an Orthodox religious celebration at Worcester's Memorial Auditorium in the 1960s. The auditorium was used to host the Sunday of Orthodoxy services that brought area Orthodox churches of different jurisdictions together for one service in the city. This was done under the auspices of the Council of Eastern Orthodox Churches of Central Massachusetts, which was founded in 1955. (WHM.)

Rev. Solon Tsandikos gives the sacrament of Holy Communion to a newly baptized infant in this 1966 photograph. In the Eastern Orthodox Church, the baptism of infants includes full immersion in water, followed by chrismation, then Holy Communion. Thus, the infant has three sacraments in one service. (WHM.)

From left to right, Penelope E. Bitzas, Loukia S. Bitzas (née Sarando), Theresa B. Sampson (née Boulmetis), and an unidentified woman decorate the *kouvouklion* on Great and Holy Friday morning. This elaborate canopy, made of wood or metal, represents Christ's tomb. The *Epitaphios*, an embroidered cloth icon depicting the dead body of Christ, is laid in the *kouvouklion*. The *kouvouklion*, richly decorated with flowers, is processed outside the church. (WHM.)

A young girl crawls underneath the *kouvouklion* during the services of Great and Holy Friday. This is done by some as a ritual for cleansing, healing, and purification, symbolizing the following of Christ into the tomb and thus into death. On the *solea* is the 12-foot double-headed eagle, the symbol of the Byzantine Empire, made of colored terrazzo. It was donated by Angelus Cotsidas and Theodore Tonna. (WHM.)

Rev. Dean N. Paleologos (foreground) and Rev. Dr. Emmanuel Clapsis (behind Reverend Dean) process the *Epitaphios* around the *kouvouklion* during the afternoon service known as the *Apokathelosis*, or Vesper Service of Great Friday. In this service, Christ is taken down from the cross, and the *Epitaphios* is placed in the *kouvouklion*. Altar boy Christopher J. Helali (at right) leads the priests, censing the *Epitaphios* with the *katsion*, or hand censer. (HKN.)

Archbishop Iakovos of North and South America (left) points to a plaque honoring Angelus Cotsidas (center) and Theodore Tonna, who stand proudly next to him. This picture was taken in early May 1965. Cotsidas and Tonna started the Table Talk Pastry Company in 1925. Table Talk Pies eventually grew into a large company producing over a million pies a week and employing Greeks in the area. (WHM.)

Pictured here are Constantinos "Constant" A. Pantos (left) and Bishop John Joseph Wright, the first Catholic bishop of the Diocese of Worcester, who served from 1950 to 1959. He then served as bishop of Pittsburgh from 1959 to 1969. In 1969, Wright was elevated to the rank of cardinal by Pope Paul VI and became Prefect of the Congregation for the Clergy. Wright was socially liberal on issues like civil rights and criticism of the Vietnam War but theologically conservative. (JW.)

This c. 1946 image shows a meeting of a Roman Catholic and Greek Orthodox bishop. The churches in a new land allowed for ecumenical exchange and dialogue that finally led to the Catholic-Orthodox Joint Declaration of 1965. From left to right are Andrew Godimis, John Tsouros, Roman Catholic bishop Thomas M. O'Leary of Springfield, Metropolitan Panteleimon of Argyrokastro, Vlassis Kentros, and George Labovites. (WHM.)

Revs. Dean Paleologos and Nicholas Krommydas led a pilgrimage of St. Spyridon parishioners from Worcester to Jerusalem around 1984 or 1985. The importance of pilgrimage to Jerusalem was even more important during the Ottoman Empire, when it was viewed in a similar light to the hajj, the annual Muslim pilgrimage to Mecca. This is why some Greek last names have the prefix "hadji" or "hatzi"—to denote pilgrimage to Jerusalem. (HKN.)

Angeliki (left) and Panagiotis Kasidakos (right) joined Patriarch Diodoros of Jerusalem (center) for a photograph in the headquarters and residence of the patriarch in East Jerusalem, Occupied Palestine, in 1993. Patriarch Diodoros was born Damianos G. Karivalis on the island of Chios in 1923. He was the Eastern Orthodox Patriarch of Jerusalem from 1980 to 2000. (HKN.)

Revs. Dean Paleologos and Nicholas Krommydas led a pilgrimage of St. Spyridon parishioners from Worcester to the Holy Land in 1993. Here, the pilgrims are pictured with Patriarch Diodoros of Jerusalem in the patriarchal headquarters. During the pilgrimage, parishioners visited multiple sites in Jerusalem, the Occupied West Bank, and beyond. (HKN.)

Five

St. Spyridon Greek Orthodox Cathedral

This is an architectural rendering of the front view of St. Spyridon Greek Orthodox Church and the community center. In 1950, architect Christopher P. Kantianis of Springfield, Massachusetts, submitted a design for a church with a 600-person seating capacity and an auditorium below the church. His design was selected by the St. Spyridon Building Fund Committee and then sent out for bids; R.L. Whipple Company submitted the lowest bid and was awarded the building contract. (WHM.)

This photograph depicts the incorruptible body of St. Spyridon on the island of Kerkyra (Corfu). St. Spyridon was born in Cyprus and participated in the First Ecumenical Council of Nicaea (325 AD). He died in 348, and when his relics were exhumed a few centuries later, during the Arab invasion of Cyprus, he was found to be incorruptible. His relics were taken to Constantinople and, after 1453, transferred to Kerkyra. (HKN.)

George Tsagarelis (left) is pointing to the blueprints of St. Spyridon Greek Orthodox Church; Theodore Tonna is at right. The St. Spyridon Building Fund Committee was reorganized into a seven-man committee in April 1950. The committee consisted of Tonna as chairman, Ernest Andreson (Anastasios Androutsopoulos) as assistant chairman, Tsagarelis as treasurer, John Tsouros as secretary, Charles Kotsilimbas Davis as councilman, Angelus Cotsidas as councilman, and John Alexander as councilman. (WHM.)

The St. Spyridon Building Fund Committee finalized and signed the contract with the builders on October 23, 1950. Construction began immediately with an *Agiasmos* led by Bishop Ezekiel of Nizaianzos, Rev. Athanasios Rizos, and other clergy on November 12, 1950. This photograph from the spring of 1951 shows the progress made in constructing the church's foundation. In the background are the three-deckers and Park Congregational Church on Elm Street. (WHM.)

This photograph taken from Russell Street on March 10, 1951, shows the ongoing foundation work of St. Spyridon from the front of the future church. In the background are the rows of three-deckers on Elm Street and the three-decker homes located at 115 and 113 Elm Street behind the church site. (WHM.)

This photograph was taken from Elm Street on March 17, 1951, and shows the rapid progress of construction now that winter was nearly over. Various construction materials—including steel beams, bricks, and concrete blocks—are visible as masonry work is underway. In the background are Elm Park and the DeWitt house, which served as the parish house until it was demolished to make way for the community center. (WHM.)

This photograph taken on March 25, 1951, shows the crane that placed the steel beams that form the skeleton of the nave, or central part, of the church. The construction site is covered in a light dusting of snow. The clock on the Park Congregational Church shows 9:55 a.m. The masonry work has advanced from what is shown in the previous image, and the difference between the church building and the auditorium below it has become apparent. (WHM.)

This photograph of the construction site of St. Spyridon Greek Orthodox Church was taken on the corner of Elm and Russell Streets on March 25, 1951. The large trees lining the sidewalk were eventually be cut down to enhance the sidewalk and area around the church bordering the street. The sign on Russell Street states that commercial vehicles over one ton are excluded from using the street. (WHM.)

The steel beams for the central dome have been placed into position, as have the initial steel beams for the belltower, in a photograph taken near the corner of Russell and Elm Streets on April 9, 1951. The masonry work has also progressed, increasing in height. Ropes and cables are visible on various sides of the church building. (WHM.)

From left to right, Rev. Athanasios Rizos, Thomas Kaplanes, and George Tsagarelis pose in front of the St. Spyridon construction site for a photograph taken by George Cocaine in the spring of 1951. Kaplanes was a member of the board of the "Enosis" Epirotic Society of Worcester in the 1950s. (WHM.)

This is a view of the ongoing construction of St. Spyridon Greek Orthodox Church from Russell Street on May 4, 1951. The masonry has progressed beyond where the stained-glass windows will go. The windows, in pairs of three, can be seen on both sides of the nave. The crane is located on the Elm Street side of the construction site. Piles of bricks are visible in the foreground. (WHM.)

Rev. Athanasios Rizos looks at the photographer during the St. Spyridon cornerstone-laying ceremony on May 13, 1951. The ceremony was delayed due to winter weather, since construction began in November 1950. Also in the photograph are Bishop Ezekiel of Nazianzos, Angelus Cotsidas, and Charles Kotsilimbas Davis. The ceremony took place on the *solea*, and the sanctuary's apse is under construction in the background. (George Panagiotopoulos.)

Approximately 400 parishioners, distinguished guests, and visitors attended the cornerstone-laying ceremony. This picture shows the faithful gathered under the steel structure of the nave and dome. The three-decker at 115 Elm Street is in the background. Cables and ropes are still connected to the steel beams on the construction site. The lower left corner displays the beginning of electrical work on the site. (WHM.)

This picture, taken above the nave, shows a bird's-eye view of the cornerstone ceremony, which, at this point in the service, was taking place below the dome area on what would be the *solea* of the new church. Bishop Ezekiel stands in front of the table, which has on top of it the cornerstone to be ceremonially blessed and placed. Five priests and a deacon are also visible. (WHM.)

Bishop Ezekiel holds the cornerstone along with George Tsagarelis (on his right) and a young boy who also has a $10 bill in hand. To the left of Bishop Ezekiel is Theodore Tonna, and Rev. Athanasios Rizos is to the left of Tonna. Charles C. Fourkas is at far left (looking at the photographer) and has a camera hanging from his right wrist. (WHM.)

From left to right, Bishop Ezekiel, George Tsagarelis, Theodore Tonna, Charles Kotsilimbas Davis, and Ioannis Labovitiades hold two masonry trowels with mortar or concrete. The board of directors of the Greek community included Tsagarelis as president, Tonna as vice president, and Labovitiades as a board member. (George Panagiotopoulos.)

Scaffolding rises into the future dome area as extensive progress in the construction is visible at the church site in this photograph taken on July 23, 1951. The masonry work has continued all the way up to the roofline, and the apse above the altar is complete. Also visible are the raised areas that will become the *solea* and sanctuary. (WHM.)

The outside masonry work of the St. Spyridon church shows extensive progress made all the way up to the roof in this photograph taken from Russell Street (looking toward Elm Street) on July 23, 1951. Wooden scaffolding surrounds the church all the way up to the roof. The steel beams of the dome area are rising above the structure that surrounds it. (WHM.)

This photograph from the fall of 1951 includes, from left to right, (first row, seated) Eleni Rizos, unidentified girl, Nikolaos Rizos, and Ioannis Rizos; (second row, standing) unidentified woman, Catherine Tsagarelis (née Angelopoulos), architect Christopher Kantianis, Bishop Demetrios T. Makris, George Tsagarelis, Presbytera Panagiota Rizos, Rev. Athanasios Rizos, and Joanna Tsandikos (née Tsagarelis). Reverend Makris was consecrated bishop of the Titular See of Olympus on September 14, 1951. Prior to this, he served as chancellor of the Greek Orthodox Archdiocese of North and South America. (WHM.)

From left to right, architect Christopher Kantianis, Rev. Athanasios Rizos, Bishop Demetrios T. Makris, George Tsagarelis, Catherine Tsagarelis (née Angelopoulos), Joanna Tsandikos (née Tsagarelis), and Presbytera Panagiota are shown in the fall of 1951. The St. Spyridon church structure has a roof, and the bell tower is nearly complete with only the dome missing. The steel beams in the front of the church would serve as supports for the loft area. (WHM.)

This photograph from September 13, 1951, shows the side of the church nearly complete and the dome work well underway on top. Scaffolding extends from the ground level up the roof and the dome section. The distinctive brickwork of the church is contrasted with the large concrete sections that comprise the auditorium and additional spaces beneath the church. (WHM.)

The dome of St. Spyridon was modeled after the dome of Hagia Sophia in Constantinople. Constructed of gunite, the 8,000-pound dome measures 34 feet in diameter. It was specially cast and lowered into place. The liturgical east end of the building reveals the nearly completed apse, a semi-circular or polygonal recess in a church where the altar is located. This picture was taken on October 16, 1951. (WHM.)

Workers guide the dome of the bell tower as it is lowered into place by a large crane on November 30, 1951. Wooden scaffolding still surrounds the church, and a ladder has been placed from the roof to the top of the bell tower. The roof has also had additional work done to it, though the tiles have yet to be placed. (WHM.)

The construction on the inside of the church is shown in this picture from March 10, 1952. Three workers are sitting and taking a rest on the *solea*, while another two workers are standing on the sanctuary's steps. Buckets, bags, and various tools are visible on the floor. The outlines of the architectural motifs and medallions and the raised Greek text on the dome are visible. (WHM.)

George Cocaine took this photograph of the nearly completed church on March 25, 1952. The dome's white color prominently stands out against the red tile roof. Most of the church's exterior work had been completed by this point. On the roof, a worker is setting the cross at the front of the church. (WHM.)

The church opened its doors on Palm Sunday, April 13, 1952. Bishop Ezekiel of Nazianzos officiated at this service along with Rev. Athanasios Rizos and other clergy from the area. Icons and other liturgical items were moved from the Orange Street church into the new church. The internal work of the church was still incomplete at this time. (WHM.)

Rev. Athanasios Rizos (left), an unidentified man, and Bishop Ezekiel of Nazianzos (right) stand in front of the sanctuary of St. Spyridon Greek Orthodox Church on Russell Street. The unidentified man holds the key to the new church, which opened on April 13, 1952. Of note are the missing iconostasis and stained-glass windows on the apse. (WHM.)

The church is shown from the front in this photograph taken by George Cocaine on March 25, 1952. The icon of St. Spyridon above the main doors at the entrance of the church had yet to be placed. On the left side of the front entrance are a cross and the words "St. Spyridon Greek Orthodox Church" in stainless steel. (WHM.)

Above the entrance of the church is the completed icon of St. Spyridon, donated in memory of George Alexander, one of the building committee members. Above the doors, in Greek, is the first line of the 83 Psalm of David, which translates to, "How amiable are Thy Tabernacles, O Lord of Hosts." This photograph was taken by George Cocaine in the spring of 1952. (WHM.)

Bishop Ezekiel of Nazianzos, flanked by the flags of Greece and the United States, leads the first service to open the newly constructed St. Spyridon Greek Orthodox Church on Palm Sunday, April 13, 1952. Rev. Athanasios Rizos is joined by another priest as well as a deacon, altar boys, and a choir. The Park Congregational Church is in the background. (WHM.)

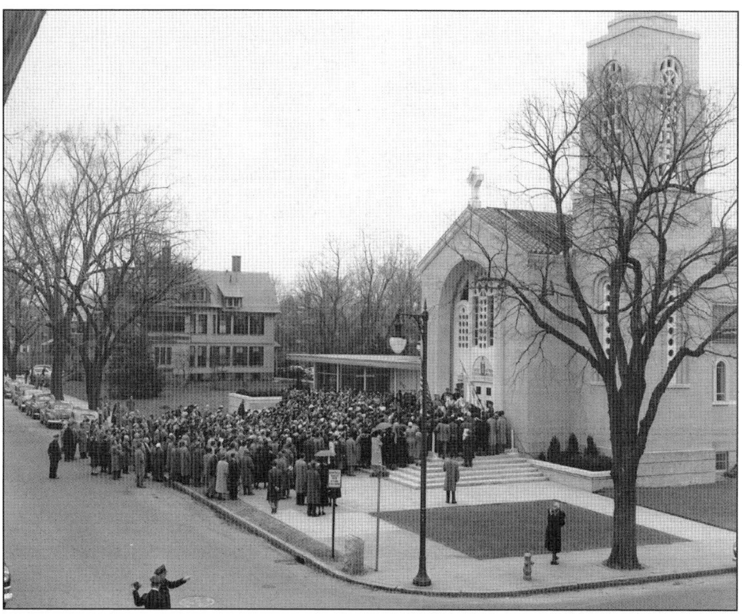

The opening service of St. Spyridon is shown from a neighboring three-decker house. This bird's-eye view shows the parishioners gathered on the steps of the church along with the clergy. In the distance is the DeWitt house, the new parish house of the church community, where the procession for the opening of the church began. (WHM.)

From left to right, Angelus Cotsidas, Ernest Andreson, two unidentified men, Christopher Kantianis (architect of the newly constructed church), Ioannis Pialtos, Theodore Tonna, and Konstantinos Bokolos stand in front of St. Spyridon Greek Orthodox Church in the spring of 1952. In the background is the DeWitt house. (WHM.)

A craftsman works on the marble bishop's throne, which was donated by Charles and John Kotsilimbas Davis. All the marble in the church is white Carrara marble cut and imported from Carrara, Italy, by the Galassi-Hutton Marble Company of Boston. Many have claimed it is the best white marble available. This photograph was taken by George Cocaine. (WHM.)

The *iconostasion* was shipped in pieces from Italy and assembled by expert craftsmen. On the right are icons of Jesus Christ, St. John the Baptist, and the Archangel Michael. On the left are icons of the *Hodegetria* (Theotokos with Christ child), St. Spyridon, and the Archangel Gabriel. The *iconostasion* was donated by the families of Theodore Tonna and Angelus Cotsidas. This photograph was taken by George Cocaine. (WHM.)

The left-side marble icon stands in the narthex, depicting the *Hodegetria* in a photograph taken by George Cocaine. The marble work in the church, as well as the stained-glass windows and large chandelier, were created by craftsman John DiNatale. This icon stand was donated in memory of Neoclis and Vasilios Coris. (WHM.)

The dome rises 65 feet above the ground, giving the impression that it is floating in the air—a hallmark of Byzantine architecture. Depicted is the Last Judgment, with the inscription below it taken from the Gospel of John 4:24. On the four pendentives are the icons of the four evangelists. Suspended from the dome is an Italian-made chandelier crafted from Bohemian cut glass with 80 bulbs. (WHM.)

According to tradition, St. Spyridon still walks the island of Kerkyra performing miracles and helping those in need. As a result, there is a ritual changing of his slippers on his relics every year. These slippers, now relics themselves, were given to St. Spyridon Greek Orthodox Church in Worcester from St. Spyridon Church in Kerkyra. (WHM.)

Rev. Athanasios Rizos (left), Bishop Demetrios T. Makris of Olympus (center), and Charles Kotsilimbas Davis stand by the marble bishop's throne. In the background are the organ and 26 chimes, which were donated by the "Horos tou Zalongou" Ladies Epirotic Society of Worcester. The right side of the pews were originally used by the choir. The back of the bishop's throne served as a podium for the choir director. (George Panagiotopoulos.)

From left to right, George Tsagarelis, Bishop Demetrios T. Makris of Olympus, Rev. Athanasios Rizos, and Theodore Tonna are burning the mortgage of the church after it was fully paid off in the late 1950s. The overwhelming generosity of the Greek community allowed for the construction of the church and the adornment of its interior. Hundreds of thousands of dollars were collected in donations and gifts. (WHM.)

The growth of the St. Spyridon community necessitated more space. Christopher Kantianis designed a community center that, after redesigns, cost $300,000. The community raised half of the funds; the other half was matched by Angelus Cotsidas and Theodore Tonna. The community center opened on May 7, 1965. It has names engraved on the outside, including Socrates, Plato, Aristotle, Archimedes, Pythagoras, Homer, Aeschylus, Democritos, Hippocrates, Sophocles, Lycurgos, and Euripides. (WHM.)

St. Spyridon Greek Orthodox Church and the new community center are shown in this raised view from the corner of Russell and Elm Street. This photograph was taken by George Cocaine in the mid-to-late 1960s. The winter weather is apparent, with snow piled up along the streets and sidewalks. (WHM.)

George Tsagarelis (farthest left) shows a matted picture of St. Spyridon Greek Orthodox Church to, from left to right, Archbishop Michael of North and South America, Archbishop Athenagoras (Kavadas) of Thyateira and Great Britain, and Ernest Andreson during the church's consecration weekend, held from May 28 through May 30, 1954. The consecration program included vesper services, a dedication ball at Worcester Auditorium, and a dedication banquet at Putnam & Thurston's. (WHM.)

Ribbons were worn by the chairs of various committees for the consecration program at St. Spyridon Greek Orthodox Church. This blue-and-white ribbon belonged to Helen Pantos, who served as cochair of the Vesper Service Invitations Committee. The ribbon includes the date of the consecration—May 30, 1954. (JW.)

Six

World War II and the Greek Civil War

This photograph from the early 1940s shows a damaged Messerschmitt Bf 109 of the Luftwaffe's 52nd Fighter Wing at the airfield located on the plain between Molaoi and Sykia. In the background are Bf 109 fighters and the village of Sykia. This was one of the Luftwaffe's forward airfields that launched sorties during the Battle of Crete in 1941 and the German campaign in North Africa. (Tasos Anastasakis.)

This poster painted by Antonis Kanas for the 120th anniversary of the start of the Greek War of Independence (March 25, 1821) depicts a young man of the National Youth Organization (EON). EON was the youth wing of the 4th of August Regime under the rule of Gen. Ioannis Metaxas. The Metaxas regime has been characterized as fascist, ultranationalist, anticommunist, and corporatist. (Hoover Institution Library & Archives, Stanford University.)

In this photograph, a German soldier walks by Messerschmitt Bf 109's while an airplane lands in the distance at the German airfield near Molaoi. In the background are the villages of Molaoi and Pakia. This Luftwaffe airfield had various warplanes stationed there, including Bf 109s and Stuka dive-bombers, which took part in active combat during the military campaigns in the Balkans and North Africa. (Tasos Anastasakis.)

Angelos Alexakis (left) and Yiorgos Kasidakos, brother of Panagiotis Kasidakos, are pictured in the early or mid-1940s. Both Yiorgos (nom de guerre boulehani) and Angelos were partisans in the 3rd Battalion, 8th Regiment of the Greek People's Liberation Army (ELAS) in Parnona. Yiorgos was brutally executed with 31 other communist political prisoners in Gytheio by monarcho-fascist forces on March 21, 1947. (Eleni Alexakis.)

The National Liberation Front (EAM) produced literature aimed at both the people of Greece and at Axis soldiers stationed in Greece. In this example, EAM-ELAS addresses German soldiers directly in German. This leaflet states, "German Soldiers! Hitler is leading Germany towards catastrophe! Give your weapons to ELAS! Fight with ELAS against Hitler!" German soldiers brutally massacred unarmed Greek civilians in Kalavryta, Distomo, and numerous other villages. (HKN.)

On May 30, 1941, Manolis Glezos and Apostolos (Lakis) Santas ascended the Acropolis and tore down the Nazi swastika that flew above it. The Nazis condemned them to death in absentia, but their identities were unknown. This 1951 postcard from Socialist Bulgaria praises Glezos for that action a decade earlier and for being on hunger strike in prison in solidarity with the Greek people struggling against Anglo-American imperialism. (HKN.)

During World War II, Manolis Glezos was captured, tortured, and imprisoned on three different occasions by the German, Italian, and Greek collaborationist forces. He was imprisoned and sentenced to death during the Greek Civil War. This postcard from Socialist Bulgaria depicts a handcuffed Manolis standing on top of the Nazi flag in front of the Parthenon. The Bulgarian subtext reads, "Freedom to the national hero of Greece—Manolis Glezos." (HKN.)

Following the German invasion of Greece, the Communist Party of Greece (KKE) built a network of resistance groups, eventually creating the National Liberation Front (EAM), the largest resistance movement in Greece. While playing a leading role, KKE formed a committee of various left-wing and liberal organizations to lead EAM. This EAM pamphlet entitled "Program of People's Democracy" was printed by the Central Committee of EAM in Athens in 1945. (HKN.)

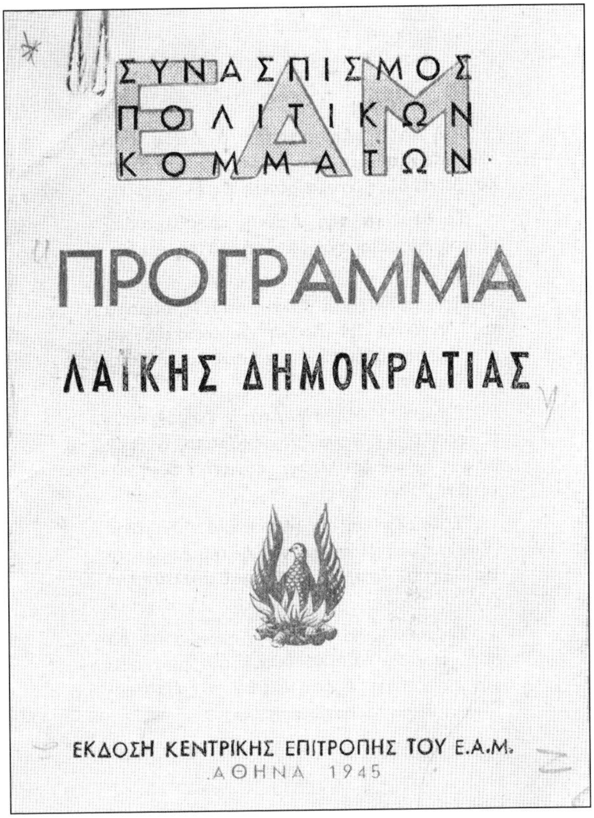

EAM formed a government in the liberated areas of Greece in opposition to the Nazi collaborationist government in Athens and the Greek government-in-exile in Cairo. The Political Committee of National Liberation (PEEA), also known as the "Mountain Government," governed most of Greece in 1944. PEEA issued this 5 *oka* (1 *oka* equals 1.282 kg) bond note, valued in wheat, to provide a stable exchange rate given Greece's hyperinflation. (HKN.)

The United Panhellenic Organization of Youth (EPON) was the youth wing of the National Liberation Front (EAM). It operated in Axis-occupied Greece but was declared illegal in 1947. It operated illegally until the Communist Party of Greece (KKE) formally dissolved it in 1958. Panagiotis Kasidakos was a member of EPON during World War II. This EPON poster from the 1940s shows a young man holding a bolt-action rifle and states "we fight and we sing." (HKN.)

The USSR, the United Kingdom, and the United States fought against fascism as allies during World War II. The National Liberation Front (EAM), however, distrusted the United States and United Kingdom. British and right-wing paramilitary groups in Greece turned on EAM-ELAS, culminating in the *Dekemvriana* and the start of the Greek Civil War—the first conflict of the Cold War. The Communist Party of Greece (KKE) dissolved EAM-ELAS, replacing it with the Democratic Army of Greece (DSE) which fought both monarcho-fascism and Anglo-American imperialism. (HKN.)

The Axis invasion and occupation of Greece severely impacted an already fragile Greek economy. Declining revenue and the lack of taxation to cover government expenditures, precipitated by a catastrophic fall in national income, led to an extreme period of hyperinflation. The Greek government-in-exile returned in October 1944 and enacted a stabilization program. This banknote for 2,000 million (or 2 billion) drachma was printed in Athens on October 11, 1944. (HKN.)

From October 1944 to November 1944, Greece experienced one of the most acutely devastating periods of economic hyperinflation in world history. According to the Hanke-Krus Hyperinflation Table, Greece ranks sixth behind (in order) Hungary, Zimbabwe, Yugoslavia, Republika Srpska, and Germany for the worst hyperinflation rate ever experienced. The 100-billion-drachma banknote depicted here, printed in Athens on November 3, 1944, is the largest denomination Greece ever produced. (HKN.)

Nikos Zachariadis was the general secretary of the Communist Party of Greece (KKE) from 1931 to 1956. Born in the Ottoman Empire, he and his family were forcibly relocated to Greece in 1922. He studied in the USSR and later was arrested by the Metaxas dictatorship. Zachariadis was transferred to the Dachau concentration camp in 1941 and released in May 1945. Zachariadis led the Communist Party of Greece (KKE) during the Greek Civil War. (HKN.)

This postcard from Socialist Bulgaria depicts a female Democratic Army of Greece (DSE) fighter with a bolt-action rifle and garrison cap with the delta insignia on the cap referring to the Greek word *demokratia*, or democracy. The fighter is contrasted with a Hellenistic statue, likely the Venus de Milo, that shows both the continuity of beauty and the embodiment of the Greek national spirit from antiquity to the partisans. (HKN.)

The Greek Civil War plunged the country into violence, hunger, and poverty once more. In its first use since World War II, American-supplied napalm was deployed by the Greek Air Force in operations against the Democratic Army of Greece (DSE). Deteriorating relations between the West and the USSR led to DSE's defeat in 1949. Thousands of children were evacuated to socialist countries in what is known as the *paidomazoma*. (HKN.)

Manolis Glezos visited the USSR in 1957 to celebrate the 40th anniversary of the Great October Socialist Revolution. Glezos was imprisoned in Greece in 1958, and the USSR released a stamp in 1959 demanding his freedom. After he was released from prison in 1962, Glezos traveled to the USSR in 1963 to be awarded the Lenin Peace Prize. This postcard from the USSR shows Manolis and his wife, Georgia, and their son Nikos on Red Square in front of Lenin's mausoleum. (HKN.)

Following the Greek Civil War, right-wing forces attempted to dominate Greek politics. The political crisis devolved into a military coup d'état against the constitutional monarchy by right-wing colonels who established a fascist military junta known as the Regime of the Colonels. The junta was defined by anticommunism, fascist ideology, and the rehabilitation of Nazi collaborators of the security battalions, or *germanotsoliades*. The junta fell in July 1974. (Library of Congress.)

The Socialist Labor Party of Greece (SEKE) was founded on November 4, 1918, following the October Revolution in Russia. With the ascendancy of Lenin and the Bolsheviks, SEKE affiliated with the Comintern and changed its name to the Communist Party of Greece (KKE) in 1924. It was banned in 1936 and finally legalized after the junta. These KKE dues stamps and coupons show the change from drachmas to euros. (HKN.)

Seven

Politics and Civic Life

Prince Paul of Greece is seated surrounded by members of Worcester's Greek community in a photograph dated February 1926. Prince Paul, in exile from 1923 to 1935, arrived in the United States in 1925. He lived with his cousin Princess Xenia Georgievna of Russia and her husband, William B. Leeds Jr., on Long Island. He traveled around the United States before departing for Europe on Cunard's RMS *Berengaria* in March 1926. (WHM.)

Charles Kotsilimbas Davis (standing in the middle, facing the camera) is shown with a group of men presenting a bust to Pres. Franklin Delano Roosevelt in the Oval Office at the White House. Roosevelt became an AHEPA member of Delphi Chapter 25 in 1932. Davis was president of Putnam and Thurston's Restaurant in Worcester for many decades; he also had the opportunity to also meet Lyndon B. Johnson and Richard Nixon. (WHM.)

Leonidas Kasidakos, the father of Panagiotis Kasidakos, stands with three of his grandchildren—Leonidas Tsiotras (left), Paraskevi Helali (center), and Paraskevi Tsiotras—in a photograph taken in Greece at Christmas time in the 1960s. Note the large photograph of US president John F. Kennedy in the background. Kennedy was beloved as a peacemaker who sought to bring an end to the Cold War. Many people believe the CIA was responsible for Kennedy's assassination. (HKN.)

Worcester mayor Andrew B. Holmstrom (fifth from left) presents keys to Helen Boufidis (third from left) and Daria Coscoros (fourth from left), the daughters of Mayor Stamatios A. Desyllas of Kerkyra, Greece, in a photograph from 1952. Stamatios served as mayor from 1951 until his death in 1955—a year after his reelection. His wife, Maria Desylla-Kapodistria, was elected after his death, making her the first woman elected mayor of a city in the history of modern Greece. (JW.)

Constantinos Pantos (left) and Angelus Cotsidas (center) pose with an unidentified woman holding a key to the city of Worcester in a photograph dated October 6, 1957. During World War II, Cotsidas was the chairman of Greek War Relief in Worcester. Throughout the war, the Greek community held events to support the struggle, including a banquet thrown on December 12, 1943, in honor of Adm. Alexander Sakellariou of the Greek Navy. (JW.)

Worcester mayor Andrew B. Holmstrom (left) and Constantinos Pantos hold two replica Greek amphorae. They were gifted to the city by Stavros B. Theofanidis of Athens, Greece, in appreciation of the hospitality shown to him while he was visiting Worcester in 1942. Holmstrom served as mayor of Worcester from 1950 to 1953. (JW.)

Worcester mayor James D. O'Brien (right) and Constantinos Pantos hold a fifth-century BC Greek figurine. Gen. Pafsanias Katsotas, the mayor of Athens, gifted the statue to Pantos, who in return gave the general a key to the city of Worcester. Pantos then gave the statue to Mayor O'Brien, who donated it to the Worcester Art Museum. Accompanying Pantos was Peter Cotsidas, the brother of Angelus Cotsidas. (JW.)

From left to right are Andreas Papazisis, Constantinos Pantos, Joseph D. Ward, and Andrew A. Godimis. This 1960 photograph shows Pantos shaking hands with Ward, the Massachusetts secretary of the commonwealth from 1959 to 1961. Ward represented Worcester's 13th District in the Massachusetts House of Representatives from 1949 to 1956. He went on to represent Worcester's 3rd District in the Massachusetts Senate from 1963 until his retirement in 1973. (JW.)

Joseph D. Ward (left) points to the state flag of Massachusetts as Constantinos Pantos holds it open to display the state coat of arms. Ward gave the flag to Pantos, who presented it to representatives of Archbishop Makarios III, president of the Republic of Cyprus. Archbishop Makarios, who was dubbed the "Castro of the Mediterranean," wrote a letter thanking Constantinos for his trip and support for "Cyprus's sacred liberation struggle." (JW.)

In this photograph taken by Marvin Richmond, Constantinos Pantos (left) joins Mayor Joseph C. Casdin of Worcester (right) as the mayor signs a proclamation for Greek Independence Day on March 25, 1959. Casdin, a member of the Democratic Party, served three terms (1959, 1962–1963, and 1967–1968) as mayor of Worcester and made history by becoming the city's first Jewish mayor. Casdin also served on Worcester's city council from 1956 to 1982. (JW.)

Theofanis George Peepas (left) was presented with the key to the city of Worcester by Paul Vincent Mullaney (right) in 1967. Mullaney was mayor of Worcester from 1963 to 1965, a Worcester city councilor from 1960 to 1967, and was then appointed as a district court judge in Worcester County. During World War II and the Korean War, Mullaney was a Marine Corps officer and was highly decorated for bravery. (WHM.)

Eight

Social, Fraternal, and Philanthropic Organizations

This c. 1917 photograph shows the men of the St. George's Hellenic Benefit Society of Tsamanta. Over 100 men from Tsamanta arrived in the United States in the early 20th century. Early arrivals worked as fruit peddlers, dishwashers, cooks, bakers, and in other low-wage jobs. Many of the men saved money and were known for being thrifty, helping them to be able to send funds to support their families in Tsamanta. (WHM.)

This c. 1950 photograph shows the members of St. George's Hellenic Benefit Society of Tsamanta. By the early 1970s, St. George's Society had approximately 350 members. Members of the diaspora and their descendants kept close ties with their village. One of the great benefactors of the Greek community in Worcester, Stavros Bellos, was a son of Tsamanta. He left millions to be divided between Tsamanta, St. Spyridon, and the Tsamanta society. (WHM.)

This image of the Banquet of the Panepirotic Society "Enosis" in Worcester is dated March 3, 1940. The Panepirotic Federation of America was founded in 1942 in Worcester. The name "Enosis," used for the local society, comes from the desire to unite Northern Epirus in Albania with Southern Epirus in Greece. The society and larger federation advocate for the rights of the Greek minority in Albania, as well as providing scholarships and grants. (WHM.)

Metropolitan Panteleimon of Argyrokastro led a North Epirotic delegation at the bequest of the Panepirotic Federation of America. The organization financially supported refugees and orphans from Northern Epirus who had resettled in Greece. Born Christos Kotokos in Korçë, Ottoman Empire, Panteleimon studied at the Theological School of Halki in Constantinople and earned a law degree at the University of Athens. Enver Hoxha expelled him from Albania in 1945. (JW.)

Greek School alumni are pictured on the front steps of St. Spyridon Greek Orthodox Church on Russell Street on November 12, 1961. The Greek School Alumni Association was formed in 1956 to promote relationships between current and former students. It was also able to provide scholarships in addition to hosting reunions and various activities. It lasted only 10 years. (WHM.)

The first Greek School students of the Greek community in Worcester were either first-generation Greek-Americans or were young when they arrived in the United States. Afterward, successive generations felt the need to teach their children the Greek language as more generations were born in the diaspora. This Greek School graduation-day picture was taken by George Cocaine in the 1950s. (WHM.)

Greek School students pose for a photograph taken by George Cocaine on their graduation day in the 1950s. The Greek School program ran in the afternoons after local schools had been dismissed. This allowed the students to study in English and then transition to Greek in the afternoon. Students who took this program seriously were able to communicate in both languages. Other local ethnic communities did the same—with varying degrees of success. (WHM.)

Nearly 120 alums attended the reunion of St. Spyridon Greek School at Fairbanks Country Club in Holden, Massachusetts, in late 1957. Charles C. Fourkas (first row, sixth from left) was chairman of the reunion committee. Helen Pantos (fourth row, fifth from right) was the secretary of the committee. In this photograph taken by George P. Cocaine, someone holds a photograph of the students with Rev. Vasilios Lokis around the late 1920s. (JW.)

Members of the Greek Orthodox Youth of America (GOYA) are pictured on a fishing trip around the late 1940s or early 1950s. One of the enduring legacies of Archbishop Michael was his foresight in organizing the youth of America in 1951. At first, young people between 14 and 18 belonged to the Olympians and Olympiads. Young adults over 18 joined GOYA. St. Spyridon is home to the Phi Sigma Theta chapter of GOYA. (WHM.)

Members of the George Jarvis Chapter No. 80 of AHEPA are shown here in the mid- to late 1920s. The chapter was formed in 1925. Charles Kotsilimbas Davis (first row, center) was the first president of the chapter. To his right is Constantine (Charles) M. Moschos. Second from left in the second row is is George Peepas, and to his left is Nicholas Petrakopoulos. (WHM.)

Members of the George Jarvis Chapter No. 80 of AHEPA celebrated 25-year members with a banquet at Putnam and Thurston's on March 15, 1953. This photograph taken by George Cocaine shows the men assembled for the festivities. The chapter was later renamed for Peter L. Bell, a longtime member and former supreme president of AHEPA from 1951 to 1953. (WHM.)

Constantine Pantos displays his 35-year pin with George Liacos (center), the president of the George Jarvis Chapter of AHEPA in Worcester, and district lieutenant governor Chris Johns (left) of Worcester in May 1968. The event honoring 25- and 35-year members of AHEPA included guests Demetrios Ritsos, the mayor of Athens, Greece; and Tasos Frantzolas, an Athens city councilor. (JW.)

The Supreme Lodge of the Order of Ahepa

Certificate for

50 YEARS OF ACTIVE SERVICE

Presented to

CONSTANTINE PANTOS

GEORGE JARVIS CHAPTER #80, WORCESTER, MASS.

In Sincere Appreciation and Recognition of his Fifty Years of Distinguished Service, Loyalty, and Devotion to his Chapter and to the Fraternity.

Date: MARCH 14, 1975

ORDER OF AHEPA

William D. Chirgotis
Supreme President

A. Steve Betzelos
Supreme Secretary

This certificate for 50 years of active service was awarded to Constantine Pantos of the George Jarvis Chapter No. 80 of AHEPA in Worcester on March 14, 1975, by the Supreme Lodge of the Order of Ahepa. Pantos was one of the 25 charter members of Worcester's AHEPA when it was founded in 1925. (JW.)

Archbishop Athenagoras of North and South America is pictured with the Ladies Philoptochos Society of St. Spyridon on Orange Street in about 1946. Archbishop Athenagoras founded Philoptochos in November 1931. The Greek community established a Worcester chapter in 1939. Archbishop Athenagoras served as Ecumenical Patriarch in Constantinople from 1948 to 1972. Patriarch Athenagoras and Pope Paul VI mutually rescinded the excommunications of 1054 while both men were in Jerusalem in 1964. (WHM.)

The Ladies Philoptochos Society prepares Paschal red eggs in 1974. Bishop Iakovos of Apameia distributed the eggs, which numbered more than 900. From left to right are (first row, seated) Theodora Panagiotou, Stephanie Tsandikos, Catherine Tsagarelis, Triada Panagiotou, Victoria Stefos, Stella Godimis, and Angeliki Serekis; (second row, standing) Evdoxia Vasiliou, Aphrodite Tsouros, Helen Pantos, Evanthia Koutoulas, Presbytera Ioanna Tsandikos, president Ekaterini Singas, Miss Kyrousis, Barbara Doukas, Effie Nicholson, Angelike Angelis, Athena Gaba, and Angelike Rassias. (WHM.)

St. Spyridon's Ladies Philoptochos Society was installed on September 13, 1981. From left to right are (first row) Theresa B. Sampson, Sandra Lano, Evanthia Koutoulas, Rev. Alexander Sgouros, Miranda Sgouros, Helen Pantos, and Georgia Stratis; (second row) Areti Biliouris, Angeliki Rassias, Victoria Cipas, Helen Mello, Athena Gabas, and Athena Stoupis; (third row) Mary Marinakis, Athena Tsoules, Victoria Stefos, Fotini Stamoulis, and Sophie Johns. (JW.)

The St. Spyridon's Ladies Philoptochos Society is shown in this 1980s photograph. From left to right are (first row, seated) Angeliki Rassias, Katherine Chipas, Evanthia Koutoulas, Rev. Dean Paleologos, Presbytera Cynthia Paleologos (née Kaloyanides), and Helen Tatsis; (second row, standing) Mary Marinakis, Helen Pantos, Theresa Sampson, Helen Mello, Mrs. Vangos, Victoria Chipas, Athena Tsoules, Evangelia Angelis (née Siova), and Sandra Lano. (WHM.)

On behalf of the Greek School alumni, Helen Pantos (right) presented cuff links emblazoned with the Chi Rho to Bishop Demetrios T. Makris (left) of Olympus at an event on April 7, 1968. Vasilios Economou, who is standing at the podium, did the announcing for the event. While serving at St. Spyridon, Bishop Makris had a profound impact on shaping the community. He moved the church toward growth and expansion, securing the Elm Street lot during his tenure as parish priest. (WHM.)

In the fall of 1981, Helen Pantos (left), the outgoing president of Philoptochos, and Evanthia Koutoulas (right), the incoming president of Philoptochos, posed on the steps of St. Spyridon Greek Orthodox Church. On October 4, 1981, the church honored the 50th anniversary of the national Philoptochos society by hosting a dinner dance at the Sheraton-Lincoln Inn. (JW.)

Nine

Community and Social Life

The St. Spyridon Greek Orthodox Church Parish Council is shown in this late-1940s image. From left to right are (first row, seated) Theodore Tonna, Ernest Andreson, Rev. Athanasios Rizos, Angelus Cotsidas, and John Kotsilimbas Davis; (second row, standing) Yiorgos Alexandropoulos, Ioannis Pialtos, Ioannis Labovitiadis, George Tsagarelis, Konstantinos Bokolos, and Charles C. Fourkas. (WHM.)

Metropolitan Panteleimon of Argyrokastro is pictured with "Enosis" Epirotic Society members at the Wayside Inn in April 1947. From left to right are (seated) Angelus Cotsidas, Constantine Moschos, Ernest Andreson, Panteleimon, Ioannis Labovitiadis, Charles (Constantine) Kotsilimbas Davis, Demetrios Andreson, Theodore Tonna, and Yiorgos Labovitiadis; (standing) Rev. Athanasios Rizos, John Tsouros, George Tsagarelis, John Pantos, Vlassios Kentros, Andrew Godimis, Harris Labovetiades, Theoharis Dallas, Nikolaos Kores, and Constantine Pantos. (WHM.)

Priests traditionally have an important social function for Greek Orthodox Christians. They attend not only religious services and functions but also national and social ones. From left to right are (seated) George Tsagarelis, Angelus Cotsidas, Rev. Athanasios Rizos, and Peter Bell; (standing) Bessie Lagadinos, Presbytera Panagiota, Joanna Tsandikos, Eva Cotsidas (née Pigoga), and Catherine Tsagarelis. (WHM.)

This picture was taken during the engagement party of Solon Tsandikos (second from right, looking at the camera) and Joanna Tsagarelis (standing next to Solon and looking at the camera). Also in this photograph are Rev. Athanasios Rizos, Angelus Kotsidas, and George Tsagarelis. Solon soon became a priest, and Joanna became a *presbytera*. On the table is a tray that looks like it may have a ring box on it. (WHM.)

Men of St. Spyridon, with cigarettes and drinks in hand, gathered for an enjoyable evening with one another, as shown in this 1950s image. George Tsagarelis is seated at far left. Also in the photograph are Chris E. Litsas, Peter L. Bell, Ioannis Pialtos, Thomas Kaplanis, and Charles Fourkas. (WHM.)

Women of St. Spyridon are pictured in the 1950s. Orthodox Christianity has a prominent place for women even if they are not allowed to be priests or bishops. If it were not for the Theotokos, there would be no incarnation and thus no salvation. That is why in Orthodox Churches there is a special icon on the altar's apse called "more spacious than the heavens," depicting the Theotokos carrying Christ in her womb. (WHM.)

These members of the Greek School Alumni Association are, from left to right, (first row, seated) Paul Liangos, Theofanis Peepas, Presbytera Panagiota Rizos, Rev. Athanasios Rizos, Pericles Labovites, and Arthur (James) Serekis; (second row, standing) George Cocaine, Madeline Dalambakis, Helen Pantos, Theresa Boulmetis, Helen Komenos, Mary Stavros Rossetti, and Charles Fourkas. This picture is from the 1950s. (WHM.)

Pictured here are, from left to right, Peter Bell, an unidentified woman, Fr. Arthur J. Rizos, Charles C. Fourkas, Charles Kotsilimbas Davis, Bessie Lagadinos, George Tsagarelis, two unidentified people, and Constantinos Pantos. According to notes written by Pantos on the back of the photograph, this bon voyage reception for Davis, Bell, Tsagarelis, and Lagadinos was held at the home of John Laureene and his wife. (JW.)

The St. Spyridon Greek Orthodox Church Basketball team posed for this picture taken by George Cocaine in the late 1950s or early 1960s. The youth of St. Spyridon started to play basketball in 1956, and it has been an important part of the church's engagement with youth and sports. The St. Spyridon team won the 2008 High School Division Championship. (WHM.)

Clergy and laity gathered for a meal in Worcester around the time of the construction of the Russell Street St. Spyridon church around the early 1950s. From left to right are (seated) Rev. Demetrios T. Makris, Theodore Tonna, Charles Kotsilimbas Davis, Bishop Ezekiel of Nazianzos, George Tsagarelis, Rev. Vasilios Lokis, Angelus Cotsidas, and Rev. Athanasios Rizos. (George Panagiotopoulous.)

Clergy, distinguished guests, leaders of the Greek community, and the faithful enjoyed a meal before George Tsagarelis was awarded the Man of the Year Award by the Ladies Philoptochos Society of St. Spyridon in 1961. Tsagarelis is at the table along with his son-in-law Rev. Solon Tsandikos, who is all the way at the end of the table on the far left side of the photograph. (WHM.)

Young girls and children with popcorn in hand sat on the park benches to watch a softball game. Bishop Demetrios T. Makris of Olympus is fifth from the left in the first row. Directly to his right is Joanna Tsandikos (née Tsagarelis). This photograph was taken in the 1950s. (WHM.)

In this 1950s photograph, Rev. Athanasios Rizos (left), Bishop Demetrios T. Makris of Olympus (center), and Pericles "Spud" Labovites play softball. Reverend Rizos is in his non-clerical clothing, while Bishop Demetrios is in his *anteri*, or inner cassock. (WHM.)

Young men and women gathered for a dance organized by St. Spyridon Greek Orthodox Church in 1958. Pictured here are, from left to right, (first row, seated) Donna Coris, Hariklia Giannopoulous, Evridiki Economou, Olive Labovites, Mina Panagiatou, Vasiliki Sahinis, and Anna Makos; (second row, standing) Mike Coris, Evangelos Giannopoulous, Polizois Economou, Vasilios Economou, Pericles Labovites, Pano Panagiatou, Leonidas Sahinis, and Dr. Athanasios Zeris. (WHM.)

Dionysius "Dennis" Tavlas (left), Bishop Silas (center), and Constantinos Pantos are pictured in June 1956. Dionysius and his wife, Athina Petralias, were from Divri (Dhivër), a Greek village in Northern Epirus that is now in Albania. Born Savas Koskinas on December 27, 1919, in Kerkyra, Bishop Silas studied at the University of Athens and arrived in the United States in 1946. He was elevated to Metropolitan of New Jersey and served as president of Hellenic College Holy Cross Greek Orthodox School of Theology. (JW.)

Helen A. Pantos (standing at far left) is shown with unidentified women in a photograph dated August 1957. Pantos was a graduate of Becker College, class of 1933. She was a social worker for the Department of Public Welfare and retired at the age of 87 after serving the department for 61 years. She was very active in the church, helped found the choir, and received the Greek Orthodox Clergy-Laity Award from Metropolitan Methodios in 1993. (JW.)

The St. Spyridon Greek Orthodox Church Parish Council is shown in 1964. From left to right are (first row, seated) unidentified cleric, George Tsagarelis, James Andreson, Angelus Cotsidas, Andrew Godimis, Theodore Tonna, and Rev. Solon Tsandikos; (second row, standing) Chris Litsas, George Montouris, Theofanis Peepas, Arthur Lagadinos, George Botsis, James Kaltsas, and James Drapos. (WHM.)

This picture of the St. Spyridon Greek Orthodox Church Parish Council was taken by George Cocaine in 1965. From left to right are (first row, seated) Theofanis Peepas, Angelus Cotsidas, Rev. Solon Tsandikos, George Botsis, Theodore Tonna, and Chris Lekas; (second row, standing) James Andreson, Chris Dionis, Chris Litsas, George Montouris, Michael Coris, Nicholas Drapos, James Kaltsas, and Andrew Godimis. (WHM.)

The St. Spyridon Greek Orthodox Church Parish Council is shown in this 1970s image. From left to right are (first row, seated) Nicholas Dodos, Nicholas Cotsidas, Rev. Solon Tsandikos, Gregory Zekos, and Thomas Drakos; (second row, standing) Paul Tsourides, Vasilios Economou, Leonidas Sahinis, James K. Davis, unidentified, Christos Liolis, unidentified, Charles Fotos, Dr. Harry Pappas, Leo Biliouris, and Chris Johns. (George Panagiotopoulos.)

The St. Spyridon Greek Orthodox Church Parish Council is pictured in the 1970s. From left to right are (first row, seated) Chris Liolis, James Zographos, Fr. Solon Tsandikos, Gregory Zekos, Nicholas Dodos, and Nicholas Cotsidas; (second row, standing) Paul Tsourides, Leo Biliouris, Thomas Drakos, Charles Fotos, Mike Kiritsy, Jimmy Economou, Pericles Demis, and George Photakis. (WHM.)

The St. Spyridon Greek Orthodox Church Parish Council is pictured in the 1970s. From left to right are Alice Christy (née Gouveris), Chris Lekas, Thomas Efthimiou, Arthus Shocas, Paul Liolios, Vasilios Economou, Philip Fotiades, Nick Petralias, Fr. George Stephanidis, Theodore Singas, Dr. Demetri Tsagronis, Heracles Biliouris, Konstantinos Economou, Jimmy Alexander, Eleftherios Stratis, and Dr. Alexandros Gouvelis. (WHM.)

The St. George Society of Douviani, Argyrokastro, Northern Epirus, founded in 1918, hosted a dinner at Nick's Grill in the 1960s. From left to right are (first row) Thomas Tsoupis, Panagiotis Panagiotou, Leonidas Sahinis, Thomas Efthimiou, Vasilios Economou, Constantine Papakosta, and Evangelos Giannopoulos; (second row) Vasilios Panagiotou, George Labovites, Michael Coris, Alexander Pallas, George Corris, John Pallas, George Pallas, Spyridon Tsoupis, and Constantine Economou; (third row) Efthemios Economou, Spyridon Panagiotou, Constantine Economou, Pantelis Panagiotou, Constantine Zangos, Demetrios Karagianis, Constantine Tzoumbas, Pericles Labovites, Philip Chicolas, Constantine Karavangelis, and Demetrios Labovites. (WHM.)

The board of directors of St. Spyridon Greek Orthodox Church are shown here around 1971. From left to right are Vasilios Economou, Paul Tsouridis, Dr. Harry Pappas, James K. Davis, Chris Johns, Chris Liolis, and Thomas Demis. Davis is the son of Charles Kotsilimbas Davis. The men are dressed for a formal black-tie event. (WHM.)

The Greek community hosts exhibits of Greek culture and heritage. From left to right are Dr. Matthew W. Panagiotu, Stasia Hovenesian, Helen Koskinas, Katherine Pappas, and Alex Drapos. In 1978, the Hellenic Arts Society was founded to promote the richness of Hellenic heritage. The society hosts film screenings, book signings, concerts, theater performances, and lectures. (WHM.)

The first St. Spyridon Greek Orthodox Church Grecian Festival was held in 1976. Under the leadership of Fr. George Stephanides, Worcester's Greek Festival was developed and modeled on the Oakland Greek Festival. This picture from 1976 shows, from left to right, Arthus Shocas, Panagiotis Kasidakos, unidentified, Nick Petralias, Nikolaos Tzoumbas, Andrew Godimis, Angelus Cotsidas, Theodore Singas, Christo Papaefstathiou, and Basil Douka. (HKN.)

Greek community members prepare meat and vegetables on skewers for kebabs in the kitchen of the St. Spyridon community center at the Grecian Festival in 1976. From left to right are (seated) Sophia Fotos, Theodoroula Panagiotou, unidentified, Olga Economou, Evdoxia Vasiliou, and Mrs. Lekas; (standing) Thomas Foutsitzis, Mrs. Angelis, Areti Biliouris, unidentified, and Spyridon Panagiotou. (WHM.)

This is the loukoumades station at the Grecian Festival in Worcester. Pictured are Evanthia Koutoulas (left), Nicholas G. Petralias (center), and Panagiotis Kasidakos. Loukoumades are balls of air-fried dough that are golden and crunchy on the outside and soft and airy on the inside. They are covered in honey, walnuts, and cinnamon. Some claim they were given as a prize to the winners of the Olympic Games in ancient Greece. (HKN.)

From left to right are Ethel Demarky, Ekaterini T. Singas (née Exarhou), Vasiliki "Bessie" Kokkinos (née Sotiriou), Paraskevi Helali, and Angeliki Kasidakos at the loukoumades station during a Grecian Festival. Vasiliki was born in Finiki, Epirus, to Nicholas and Anna Sotiriou (née Filliou). Ekaterini was born in Vrysochori Zagorio, Epirus, in 1928. Theodore and Ekaterini Singas founded the Original House of Pizza on Pleasant Street. (HKN.)

From left to right are Joseph D. Early; Theodora Rougas; unidentified; George Photakis; unidentified; Demetrios Koutoulas; Bernard Joseph Flanagan, Roman Catholic Bishop Emeritus of Worcester; Chris Dionis; Archbishop Iakovos of North and South America; Vasilios Economou; Timothy Joseph Harrington, Roman Catholic Bishop of Worcester; Emmanuel Milias; Paul Tsongas, US senator from Massachusetts; unidentified; Sara Robertson; Evanthia Koutoulas; Rev. Dean Paleologos; and unidentified. (WHM.)

Patriarch Diodoros of Jerusalem visited St. Spyridon in Worcester in the 1980s. From left to right are (first row, seated) Bishop Anthimos of Boston, Patriarch Diodoros, and Theodore Tonna; (second row, standing) Arthur Drapos, Basil Douka, James Christo, George Panagiotopoulos, Emmanuel Milias, Angelus Cotsidas, Andrew Godimis, Demitrios M. Moschos, George Photakis, Evan Tsoules, Mike Efstratios, Charles Fotos, Steve Gaba, Rev. Dean Paleologos, and Thomas Efthimiou. (WHM.)

The Ladies Philoptochos Society of St. Spyridon has contributed money and supplies to various initiatives, projects, and the needy for decades. The society contributes to OCMC, St. Basil's, HCHC, and other causes. Pictured in the late 1980s or early 1990s are, from left to right, Rev. Fr. Nicholas Krommydas, Mary Marinakis (née Korkidis), an unidentified bishop, Elpida S. Milias, Marika Kalis (née Kounadis), and Rev. Dean Paleologos. (WHM.)

Ten

Labor and Business

The Alpha Lunch Company was located at 436 Main Street in Worcester. The corporation was organized on March 9, 1916, and incorporated on March 10, 1916, under the name Alpha Lunch Company of Boston. The corporation, according to the court case *Louis C. Strates v. George Andreson*, made over $223,000 in 1922. The directors and managers included George Andreson, Charles Andreson, and William Patterson. (WHM.)

Constantine Moschos (behind the counter at right in the above image), in partnership with Chris Pappas, opened Purity Restaurant on Canterbury Street in 1920. They operated the business from 1920 to 1959. This photograph, taken in the early years of the business, shows various products for sale, including drinks, cigarettes, cigars, and ice cream. Upon arriving in Worcester, Constantine Moschos started working as a bellhop at the Coronado Hotel. After opening Purity Restaurant in 1920, Moschos and Chris Pappas had a leasehold on the Coronado Hotel from 1943 to 1946; they purchased the hotel in 1946. It was closed in 1959 due to the economic decline in Worcester. The hotel is pictured below in 1955. (Both, WHM.)

George Peepas opened Peepas Men's Shop in 1926. A tailor by trade, Peepas had opened two shops prior to this store. The shop was located at 144 Front Street on the corner of Front and Spring Streets. Peepas worked at the store until his death in August 1950. (WHM.)

Theofanis G. (left) and George Peepas are pictured in their store. Peepas Men's Shop sold men's clothing with tailoring also available. Theofanis married Euterpe "Marie" Kornenos, from Newark, New Jersey, in July 1944 at the Orange Street St. Spyridon church, and they both worked at the men's shop. After closing the clothing store, they purchased Haddad Liquors and renamed it Bancroft Liquors, relocating it to Franklin Street. (WHM.)

George Tsagarelis purchased a diner that had been in operation at 158 Southbridge Street since 1918. He transformed the diner into the iconic Coney Island Hot Dog in 1929. In 1938, major renovations were done, giving it its current Art Deco look. George Cocaine took this picture of the iconic neon sign, which shows Tsagarelis's hand holding a saucy hot dog, being lifted by a crane on June 5, 1951. (WHM.)

This photograph shows the inside of Coney Island Hot Dog. Worcesterites still carve their names into the wooden booths. George Tsagarelis's wife, Catherine, was the daughter of a restaurant owner from Bridgeport, Connecticut. George died in 1980, and Archbishop Iakovos officiated at his funeral. Catherine then ran the business with her daughter Joanna and son-in-law Rev. Solon Tsandikos until she died in 2000. Today, George and Catherine's granddaughter Kathryn Tsandikos runs the landmark business. (WHM.)

Rev. Solon Tsandikos blessed the opening of Nicholas Ernest Andreson's candlepin bowling alley in 1960. Colonial Bowling Center cost $400,000 to build and included 24 hard rock maple candlepin lanes, pin-setting machines, and a wooden telephone booth. Candlepin bowling was invented in Worcester in the 1880s. Colonial Bowling Center was open for 60 years before it closed in 2020. It was the last candlepin bowling center in the city. (WHM.)

Helen A. Pantos, daughter of Constantinos Pantos and Emilie Marggraff (born in Germany), is seated at her desk in the foreground (next to the woman on the phone) at the Board of Public Welfare in Worcester City Hall around 1947. While care for the poor was the domain of private charities and religious institutions centuries ago, the Progressive Era and New Deal changed how the US government cared for the poor. (JW.)

Constantinos Pantos is seated in the office of Pantos Travel Agency, his business located at 122 Mechanic Street in Worcester. Pantos was born around 1883 in Northern Epirus during the rule of the Ottoman Empire. He worked in Istanbul for years before coming to the United States. Admired by many, he was known in the Worcester area—by Greeks and non-Greeks alike—as the "Mayor of Mechanic Street." (JW.)

Peter (left) and Theodore Stolakis sell popcorn and peanuts at their stand outside Worcester City Hall. The brothers saved enough money over the decades to build a home in Corinth, Greece. They retired in 1957 and moved back to Corinth to live with their older brother. They comfortably lived off their social security and savings and remained proud US citizens. George P. Cocaine traveled to Corinth to interview them. (WHM.)

Angeliki Kasidakos was presented with a gift by a manager of the New England Envelope Company during a holiday party in the 1980s. Kasidakos worked as an envelope-machine operator at the company for approximately 30 years. The New England Envelope Company became a certified organization in Massachusetts on December 8, 1906. The envelope company's office was located at 237 Chandler Street. In the late 1980s or early 1990s, the company had approximately 150 employees with sales of over $10 million. (HKN.)

Panagiotis Kasidakos (right) is pictured with two unidentified coworkers in the Filene's men's department in Chestnut Hill, Newton, Massachusetts, around 1980 or 1981. Kasidakos worked as a tailor in Greece, Canada, and then at the House of Doherty in Worcester until the fall of 1976 before joining Filene's. He was a proud trade unionist. Panagiotis served Bostonians, suburban residents, and Boston College students, including Doug Flutie. This photograph was taken by Richard W. Green. (HKN.)